I0529813

"Knowing *the* Terror *of the* Lord"

("We Persuade All Men")
2 CORINTHIANS 5:11

MERIENNE LYNCH

Copyright © 2022 by Merienne Lynch

ISBN   Softcover   978-1-956998-52-8

To order additional copies of this book, contact:
Bookwhip
1-855-339-3589
https://www.bookwhip.com

This book is dedicated to

God the Father
God the Son
and
God the Holy Spirit

INTRODUCTION

Before you read this book, there are some things that need to be understood. All of the words from here on in are actual quotes from the Holy Spirit as he presented the words to me. None of them are or were something that I would write. For months I refused to write it until He revealed to me that I was called to this purpose. For the past thirty-eight years, there were things that had happened to me that I did not have even a little understanding of. Never was any of it revealed to me until I began to write this book. This is how I came to the place that even though God held things back from me, I would believe Him and write what He told me. God taught me long time ago that the only time that He holds anything back from any one of His children is when He knows that they will not believe Him.

In some places of the King James Version of the Bible (a version that some people consider so harsh), God never dealt with me according to my sins. If He had, I would be dead. There are things in the King James Version that are absolutely true according to the way they are written. The church is in for a shock before the trumpet sounds. If they do not endure correction here, they will have to endure it there. Then it would be judgment because it would be too late for correction. This world is a shadow of things to come, and I have seen glorified bodies that have gone on to meet the Lord, and they are exactly as they are here on earth except for one thing, they are heavenly and awesomely beautiful. When you look at them, you recognize exactly who they are, and every flaw in the beauty of their creation that was corrupted by the flesh is done away with. They are not spirits flying through the air like wisps of smoke or clouds. They are actual heavenly bodies that are so beautiful that you find yourself marveling at the wonder of what God has done when you leave this earth, when you are His.

As ugly as people think demons are the ugliness of death, and sin seems worse to me. I know that if a person finds themselves in a situation with their own body and mind, they have not been able to get the victory over. When they have prayed, when they have fasted, when they have done all that is within their power to overcome. The usual case is because they have not allowed the blood of Jesus Christ to do the work of freeing them of sin consciousness. The being aware of what you are doing so much that you lose focus on God's power to take over where you are. Weak in a sin consciousness, a sin awareness, or let's just say an awareness of your weakness becomes your total focus even when you fast and pray. Leave it alone and Let God do the operation and victory is yours. And I don't mean take the sin lightly. Nor do I mean ever think it will be all right if you continue. What I do mean is that you acknowledge that without His intervention, you will never succeed. Trust in His mercy and He will reach down and touch those who cannot help themselves.

There are many who do not have the capacity to do what needs to be done for their lives, these who are "poor in spirit" as my mother was, who are pressured out of measure, where their minds could no longer endure the abuse of life. For this life is difficult for some, and we are not held responsible for the things we do not know or understand. Only for what we do know and what we do understand concerning the things of God. Our abilities lie with ourselves to such a degree that only God can truly judge us. Yes, those who hold office (speaking of the church offices, those who are responsible to God for others) have a certain amount of discernment, wisdom, and judgment; but it can only go so far. For when you see that the most powerful, the highest, has not yet been able to touch certain things, that is proof that these things can only come from God.

All of my thirty-eight years of Christian life, I have only known a God of great compassion, great understanding, great love that far reaches anything that any of us have ever known. Of all I ever suffered, it was never the hand of God that caused it; always did it come from others and the enemy of our soul. My only prayer is for every soul who reads this book to enter into a place with God so that they can see, hear, and know Him as I do. The One who never fails, One who never gives up on you, One who will always be there to help you according to His love, His compassion, His infinite understanding. According to the confines of His Word, for His only limitations are the ones He put in His Word.

To this day, and each and every day of our lives, we must all strive to die daily to do His will, not ours. We need to strive daily to get where we know that we should be, for all of us know where we ought to be. For in rejecting the truth about ourselves that we know about ourselves, we are guilty before God as written in Romans 1:18-20. For the invisible things of Him from the creation of the world are clearly seen, being understood by the things that are made, even His eternal power and Godhead, so that they are without excuse. Not all of us continue to pray about it or talk to Him about it. Unless you are lacking the simplest things in the mind, there is not one person who doesn't know when they are displeasing God. For when you give your life to Christ, the Holy Spirit enters into your life and leads you if you let Him. In all of my experiences, I have found the Word to be true, that we do not go to God with everything because we do not want to know when we are wrong. John 3:21 (KJV) says, "But he that doeth truth cometh to the light that his deeds may be made manifest, that they are wrought in God." For your natural man gets in the way. The heart is exceedingly wicked, full of self-deception, and it is the greatest destroyer of your spirit. More than anything that is ever done to you, said to you or about you. Some of these words may seem so harsh of a warning, but sometimes we need them, and I know it. "This book contains My Words for our time and hour on this earth. Right here in the United States. This book I refer to as a book of love to My church. For it is My love that leads all of you to repentance; it is through My love that opportunities are given and time to make things right with Me before the moment you must face Me in eternity. As far as I am concerned, My attitude is whatever it takes to spare the spirit from destruction.

Most of this book was written before mid-2007; some of the things written in this book have come to pass by this date, which is October 3, 2008.

From the beginning of this first part to the very end of the book, these words are directly from the Lord as He spoke them to me, I wrote them; that is why there are quotation marks here at the beginning and at the end of the book. None of the words are mine; I am only the person God used to write this book. If you want to get the most out of it, read it as though the Lord is speaking to you directly, the way you should read the Bible, always keeping in mind how much the Lord loves you. So much that He is not willing to let you do anything to destroy your relationship with Him. All that is written is designed to lead you to examine yourselves and get yourself ready for the rapture.

If you read the Word of God, you would see that Jesus never spoke to the sinner harshly. He appealed to them and asked them kindly; and He spoke with patience and love, but not so with His own, or those who were ungodly and claimed to be God's. To them the Word says, "You generation of vipers, who hath warned you to flee from the wrath that is to come?" Concerning the baptism of repentance, the Word said, "Bring therefore *fruits* meet for repentance, and think not to say within yourselves that we have Abraham to our father for I say unto you that God is able of these stones to raise up children unto Abraham" (KJV). Even in the day where they walked and talked with Jesus those who claimed to believe, claimed to have God within them, they did exactly the same thing. They committed the very same error in thinking that they would escape His wrath by claiming to be saved by faith. Their works were wicked in His sight, they were evil. They were more serious than any sinner ever committed. He let the sinner go freely, knowing that when they heard about their sin, they might take the opportunity to change. But the hypocrites and the ungodly, He treated them harshly, knowing very few of them would take the opportunity to repent. He dealt with those who appeared to have God within but were empty and dead. Because He knew that they held on to believing that they were right when they were very wrong.

I want this understood plainly and without any doubt about what I Am going to say here is true. You are about to read how I visited this vessel, and she endured My glory and My terror. The way every man who claims My name will in eternity. The way Paul the Apostle endured it when he was on the road to Damascus. No matter what anyone thinks, how anyone prays, no matter how they believe, nothing can ever come back on her for what she is writing because Satan has the power to do many things; but the one thing that he cannot do is imitate My glory and My terrifying Presence. He can make you feel fear in the flesh. But as you feel fear in the flesh, you have a witness in your Spirit that it isn't Me. No matter how it tries to consume you, you know that it isn't Me. But when I come on the scene, there is no doubt that it is I the Lord. You will never be able to say it wasn't Me. Remember this, for this is important to you.

In this book is a lot of reality of scripture written in a language that anyone can understand today. You can pick it up and think you know the scriptures there, for you do not need to read. I tell you now, if this is your attitude, then you need this book because you are the one I seek to speak to.

Before I begin to reveal through this book the many things that are wrong, I want to speak about those who are right. From behind the pulpit, I hear some great voices in this nation speak out against the sins of this age. They don't misinterpret, they don't take it out of context and they don't twist anything to suit them, and they take the Word and apply it to give wisdom where to stand in this nation on anything. I personally call them great because they preach and teach to obey My commandments. There are many who don't have access to reaching millions. There are also many who are doing a tremendous job in healing the sick, delivering the oppressed, and seeing many souls saved. There are those who want to see a sweep in our nation of revival. And I want to tell you something here. This nation will have a long-awaited and prayed-for revival as soon as every heart that I have called learns how to examine itself and see where it is not right with Me. When My people who are called by My name will humble themselves and turn from their wicked ways, I will hear from heaven and heal their land. This nation is your land, and it is in terrible need to be healed.

ix

And what did I ask them to do? "Bring fruit meet for repentance." Fruit is something that begins as a seed and grows. Fruits are something that you have to cultivate and water and expose to just enough sun. Now if you were able to only name it and claim it, only able by some miracle to obtain the fruits of the Holy Spirit, there would be no reason to call them fruits. The ungodly are those who claim to have Me in their heart but they have fruits that are obviously wicked. These people became so wrapped up in believing that they could toy with Me, pretend before Me and man to have something that they do not have; they deceived themselves, deceived each other, but never Me. The greatest revival isn't how many healings or miracles are seen. My people can get that within themselves through My Spirit. Those are for the unsaved to believe, who have never heard of conversion of the soul to Jesus. *I Am speaking of the revival that changes the heart within you toward Me and gets cleansed through the blood and allows Me to continue the operation by permitting Me to create within My church a new heart, one that is faithful and upright in spirit. A spirit that will never turn away from Me.*

I Am the same today, yesterday, and forever. I hate for people to go to church and act before men like Christians, speak like Christians, and live like demons in My sight. This is one of the greatest reasons that this book is being written. To have Christ within you, you must die daily to yourself. If you don't, you take the chance of Jesus saying these words to you, "Depart from Me, ye that work iniquity, I never knew you." In that great Day of Judgment, it will be all too late to repent, it will be too late to change and repair the damage that was done through a ministry that thought they were able to claim Me without having Me, thought that they were doing My will and yet never worked out their own salvation with fear and trembling. I do not intend for that day to come to any of My children. I desire to deal with them today, for today is the day of salvation. Right now is the hour to begin to realize that when you gave your life to Jesus, you never got everything under His blood. Had you done so, all those things that you let slide by, all those things that you have permitted to think that were going to be all right with Him would have never followed you to this hour and forwarded to the judgment.

Some of you came out of deep sin. And yes, I cleansed you and even delivered you. And the moment you entered into your new life, you presumed that all of those tendencies that you had fallen into, things that you had done were gone. You went to an altar of prayer and said a sinner's prayer, and never did you go on to a personal journey with Me to work them all out. If salvation was not to be worked out, then how can I truly turn your life around? The roots that took a lifetime to grow in this world needed to die. And some of you never touched the surface. You turned around yes and faced your past life; but instead of working it out with Me, you thought, "Now I am free, and every person that ever touched my life has sinned and will answer to God." Or you thought, "Now I am righteous and holy, and whoever dares question that will answer to God." And suddenly as quickly as that, you had become stillborn. For instead of asking Me to forgive others, you cursed them; and in so doing, you cursed yourself. Only this time, you claim to know something that you know nothing about. You strove to keep your forgiveness but forgot where you began not to forgive. It comes and visits over and over, and you do not realize it is following you until you do something about it. How can you instantly change without getting into the Word? How can you take just a part of the Word and claim everything good for you in the Word without getting rid of all of the things that are wrong in you?

Some of you kneel at an altar of prayer and pray by asking God to come into your heart. And because you set yourself so high, higher than God intended you to be, you begin to judge everybody and everything. And in so doing, you bring judgment upon your own selves. You immediately bring so much upon yourselves because of lack of understanding of the kind of spirit that you were born into. And some of you leave that altar worse off than when you came.

Some of you seek God for a while, start out correctly, and soon become what you used to be, heady, high-minded, selfish, only now you seem to have power with Me. Because of my gift to you, some do not realize that the gift is not proof that your heart is right with Me. The evidence of the fruits within your personal life between you and

Me is evidence of who you are. I call many, but few are chosen, and this means that although I called many, few are obedient.

Some of you desire so much to be seen that you sit so high, and I cannot even begin to put you where you belong for you refuse to go. You keep blaming the devil for all the things that you brought upon yourself by never hearing Me. The devil laughs in your face, and My heart is broken because you have given the enemy so much power over your life. You want the signs, you want the miracles, but you refuse to go where every Christian must go, and that is on a journey to work out every root that caused you to fall. I designed it so that you will never fall. And because the journey is not easy, because it is not glorious, and because it seems to take away from you as you die to self, you get rebellious and refuse to go and do as I called you to do. Only you cover it all up and refuse to face yourself as you are.

Matthew 3:12 says, "He will burn up the chaff with unquenchable fire." How does Jesus do that? Does it seem so hard to understand? With My Word telling you that I Am a consuming fire, how hard could that be to understand? What do you think it means to be baptized with fire? Do you just skip over those scriptures because they are too hard to understand for you? Do you picture Me as a person such as yourself that surely I did not mean fire? Surely I did not mean consume. Did I? What did I mean then if I did not mean fire?

You can understand that you can burn with passion, you can burn with lust. Both can consume your whole beings. You can burn with anger, you can burn with hate, and you can burn with compassion, you can burn with love. *And you can burn with My consuming fire.* As the disciples said when Jesus talked to them, "Did not our hearts burn within us?" Would you not rather suffer your works to be burned here and not go to hell? Would you not rather endure hardship here and not in eternity? The scriptures that deal with fire should be the ones that you first work with, and help Me do an operation within your heart and mind that you will never fall."

PART I

Paul the Apostle wrote, "Knowing the terror of the Lord, we persuade men; but we are made manifest unto God and I trust also are made manifest in your consciences" (2 Corinthians 5:11 KJV).

Thus saith the Lord, "This book which I the Lord refer to as My book of love to My church, is only written through My mercy and love that lead all of you to repentance. It is through My love that opportunities and time are given to make things right with Me, before the moment that you must face Me at the Judgment. *As far as I Am concerned, and My attitude toward all things written in this book is, 'whatever it takes to spare the spirit from destruction.'*

1 Peter 4:17 and 18. "For the time is come that judgment must begin at the house of God and if it first begin at us, what shall the end be of them that obey not the gospel of God? And if the righteous scarceley be saved; where shall the ungodly and sinner appear." (KJV) Judgement is correction. While you are here on earth; it is strictly correction. Once you leave this earth it is all too late for correction. Then it is true judgment, and it is final."

I will begin with telling you about when I visited and called this vessel to write this book. It was on Easter Day of 2002. She was in her kitchen worshipping me when the presence of My Holy Spirit began

1

to pour upon her in waves of favor. She fell to her knees and basked in My Presence. She had no idea of why I was pouring out My Spirit upon her. I wanted to touch her and reach her in such a way that I knew she would be able to completely accept Me without doubt, without fear of mistakes, without having to try the spirits. So I revealed to her My Glory. To her, My Presence began to intensify until I was all-consuming and all-powerful. And she trembled within My fear with every atom of her being. And within herself she wondered why she wasn't dead. When I subsided just a little, she asked Me, 'Why am I not dead?' I told her, 'You are no different than any other of My Prophets for they have all said, "Woe is me, I am undone, for I have seen God and what man has seen God and lived?"'

To her, she could see Me right in the middle of all My glory, as Moses saw Me in the burning bush. She saw Me and heard Me speak a message to her, and these were the words that I spoke: 'I want you to write a book. I appeared to you this way because I have a message to those who call themselves My prophets. This book will be entitled *Knowing the Terror of the Lord*. Below the title, you could see "We Persuade All Men" enclosed in parentheses. The first message must be to those who call themselves My Prophets. Ask them this question, "Are you able to stand in My Presence with the glory of My Spirit and live?"' I revealed to her that I wanted it to be made known that there are those who think that they are prophets and they are destroying My Prophets and they think they are doing Me a favor. This book is being written to warn every person who will not take heed to My warnings, that I will visit them the way I did her, and will they endure the touch?

I will back up the words of My true prophets no matter what you think of them. For your opinion of Me means nothing to Me at all. I will put it this way, what she went through with Me is a warning to *all* of My prophets of how I most definitely will visit those who need corrected. I warned all of you to pray that you are worthy of the calling in which you are called. Some of you are way out of course when I speak to you. You cannot hear Me because you have allowed too much of the flesh to be in control of you. The angel of light at times in your life looks like Me, acts like Me, sounds like Me, and comes in the manner that I have always in the past come to you. But he is so subtle, with a change that you in the flesh cannot detect. And because you have not bothered to grow in the Word with such a powerful gift, you become deceived. At first a little, then slowly it all adds up and destroys what I have originally given you. Prophecy is *never* to be given strictly for comfort. Prophecy is for warning My people to turn from their wicked ways. It is also for prayer first. That plea to turn from your ways and follow Mine is the greatest call of love that there is. And some of you pray all right, but you pray for what you believe is the prophecy and for it to be fulfilled. So that you will not be found to be mistaken, you pray for it to come true. You never realize that you could be deluded through the flesh. When I reveal something to you about any individual, let alone anyone famous, it is not necessarily to tell everyone. It is first for prayer. Not prayer to bring it to pass. Prophecy is for warnings, to rebuke and exhort, so that people could have an opportunity to repent before I come before it is too late. No prophet is a prophet without the ability to warn. Comfort to those who like or support you is not true prophecy. Although comfort is something that I do use My prophets for. But I have some who do not believe in telling the truth. They see it, they feel it, but they just don't speak it out of fear. And that fear can cause you to take on the wrong thing at the wrong time, and all the while you will think it is Me.

When I give this vessel who is writing this book a 'word' for someone, then I tell her what they have been doing up until this moment, I tell of what will happen if they don't repent, and I tell what blessing will come if they do repent. Prophecy is not written in stone. It is a potential happening if you obey Me in the Word. It is inevitability if you disobey. When a soul comes to you, as a prophet, and their past seems to leap out at you, it is for *you to pray and to tell them the truth. It is for you to reveal it to them and give them an opportunity to change it through forgiveness and repentance.* You cannot take it upon yourself to believe that because their past was revealed to you, it is the individual who will not let it go. When you do that, you are making a judgment on what I have revealed to you. All you need to know is the past strives to hinder their future. But giving them a pat on the back when they need to be led to repentance is not what I intended in prophecy. Always at

3

the altar, some things are revealed in order to defeat, to overcome, to destroy, or to be revealed for repentance. When you are not deep enough in understanding, you will see only the surface of it. And what blinds your eyes is the enemy telling you that if you tell them the truth they will turn on you. Therefore, since I revealed they were that rebellious that they would do such a thing, then tell them nothing and give them *no* chance to build up and edify themselves with what you say while they are in a rebellious state. Otherwise, you are partaker of the enemy using you to destroy them.

When you claim to be a prophet, there has to be something more than just having the gift to see what is revealed to you by My Spirit when you come in contact with a soul. There has to be more than just being pulled out of drugs, alcohol, bad marriages, abuse of any kind, etc. All those things give no special rights or privileges. All those things are not the reason that you are who you are, and they are not the reason that I chose you. I chose whom I use, and so many times you get it all mixed up in your minds here on earth. As though you earned something through the things you go through. Yes, you earn some things, but you never earn the calling that comes straight from My Throne to belong to Jesus, you never earn the calling of a prophet. It is a calling, and that calling has a great price on it. I chose you, you did not choose Me. I know it has been said repeatedly, and you think that you know what I Am saying. But I tell you even now, you do not know, because had you known, you would have dug deeper and gotten closer and would not reject the truth. You would not have rejected this book. It is kin to the Bible, and it has all the attributes of the Bible in being Holy Spirit inspired. Do you? Are you truly Holy Spirit inspired? Because if you are not, what you seem to be, what you seem to have will fade away; and as you see it take flight, repent and pray that you do not lose it. This vessel writing this book did not pray for this, nor did she ask for this, and even now as she writes, this is not something that she asks Me to fulfill. She doesn't have to. Our relationship is unlike yours and so many others. She never has to ask Me to fulfill the Words that I give her. She doesn't spend her time asking Me to do anything that she may have believed, understood, or known. She knows that if

I want that, she will have it; if it is I that speaks, it will come to pass. So she makes it her business to be sure that it is I that speaks. She rests the way all of you need to rest. I Am not speaking about your special little combinations of turning My Word to be used to suit your need.

Listen to what I Am saying to you. When you as a prophet are where you need to be with Me, dead to self, dead to all that you think or feel, then I truly dwell within you; and that releases Me as I Am. There is no need to ask, for it is already clearly yours. As you read in this book how she expected Me to heal her. She did not ask; her time of asking was over. She asked for the best things. To be worthy of My gifts, to be honest, wise, and filled with integrity even to the point of death. She doesn't ever speak to Me as though I Am not there, that I do not see, that I do not know, that I do not understand. Most of the time she communicates with Me; we both know who we are and where we stand and what is to be done. No, she is not perfect. But Jesus asked many things because of those around Him. That they might believe. Jesus knew His relationship with God, and it was very close. He communed with the Holy Spirit and God the Father as One with them, never as though He was separated asking for something. Now, if as a prophet you have this kind of relationship, then you may take what she says and toss it behind you and pray for what you desire to have and expect Me to fulfill it. But if not, if this is not the kind of relationship that you have, then you must be careful. For although I have said be careful for nothing in the Word, I have also said that you touch not Mine anointed. She completely understands the separation between the man, woman, their spirits, and My Spirit. She completely understands the gifts that I give to a man and a woman. She never fears where the separation is; she sees, she knows, and she understands because I have revealed it to her. The gift is not the man, and the gift is not the woman, the gift is Me. Many of you still do not understand, but as you read I will open up your understanding. I did this that she may speak to *all of My prophets*, not one, not two, not some, but all. And if you are one of them, then I tell you even now take heed, for I Am warning you. I Am correcting you, I Am calling you to come out from where you are and get into what I Am speaking about in this book, for the time is at hand. My

5

Word is to rebuke, to exhort; it is for correction, it is for comfort, it is for all things that need to be done in all things. And if I reveal to you something negative and you do not want to speak it out of fear, which would be doubt, then don't speak it; but never comfort them with even a little Word. Never do I tell any prophet that they can't say this or they can't say that, or they will lose the soul of the person they speak to. The flesh and the enemy tell you that because the truth must be something that you completely trust to do the operation. But fear speaks first, and you then cannot speak the truth. You must learn how to overcome this. You must learn how to love and believe and accept and understand and enjoy and embrace the truth, for My Holy Spirit is the Truth! And when you speak it, you must be able to walk away from it, leaving it completely in My hands never doubting, believing always that the truth will do the operation.

Think what you want, but I gave this vessel Ezekiel, to say it whether they will hear or forbear. Many who are not seen by the world claim to be a prophet, and they are not, and they destroy many because they are looking for their self-seeking purposes. And this needs to be read by them to warn them before I move. I give every soul a chance before I move.

"Awaken thou that sleepest and I will give thee light. This is the gospel; this is the truth, and you need to hear as you have never heard before. This is the time, this is the hour to let everything go. Those who have not died to themselves, who have not picked up their cross and followed Jesus, will now have to die to themselves; they will now have to pick up their cross and follow the One they have claimed all this time. Now it becomes real. The words that are written here are life; when you receive them, they breathe life into you. These words have the power to cause you to live. All that is mentioned in this book is to one purpose: to cause you to see yourselves as you are, to cause you to turn away from where you have been and obey the Word now. I repeat now!

When I say something to you and you accept it in your shallow understanding, you miss the mark when you grab it and run with it. Because there are things about individuals that I strive to speak to you about, and you do not hear Me. Oh, it seems like you do, but you do not. My prophecies don't go against one another. And I will not lead any of My prophets to support anyone capable of destroying the helpless innocent individuals that cannot protect themselves. It is not morally within the realm of a human being to make a decision to kill an innocent child and say that I Am with them. *Therein is your key as to whom* you are listening to. I will not change My mind on crushing the heads of innocent babies or whatever other form you develop to kill. Although I Am not with those who fight and kill and destroy medical people thinking they are justified in the cause. For no cause justifies these things. A choice between a life and the baby's life is one thing. But giving a woman that is not wanting the precious being growing within her the right to kill it; this is ungodly.

My Word plainly tells you that you will not hear My Son's voice crying in the streets about anything. I will never call any prophet from another country to go against My anointed ones here in the United States. Mine anointed know that I will never support anyone who believes there is a reason to destroy a life; they know I do not operate like that. I will never call anyone in a few moments to make a judgment that I would support any person who believes that I am so evil that I would destroy and kill millions of innocents. That is not Me, and you should have known it. I Am not speaking to any one individual, I Am speaking to *many of you.* Because many of you plan to support people that think a woman has a right to choose and she does not! Only I do!

I made a promise that I will take away what you seem to have if you do not use what I have given you. I have given you the power to discern in My Word. By their fruits, you will know them; and if you support anyone that does these things and say that I Am with you, you then open the door to hurt yourself because I Am not a false prophet, I do not change the truth into a lie. I do not take the truth and make it sound as though I Am righteous because I help someone destroy a child

7

that I created. Life is in the blood. The blood of those children cry out the way Abel's blood cried out.

It is one thing if a young person *decides* they want to go to war to defend their country and you find fault with that because you don't like war. *But I give* My children the power to defend their nation whether you like it or not. I put a noble cause within the heart of the young to lay down their life for their country without questioning that country. They have a love for it. It was born in them, and it was nurtured by Me. Whether you think it is a mistake or not, I give power to do certain things. You say this country was deceived. I say don't believe what you hear. For there are those who only want to be heard, and so they claim to have the truth and obtain what they want in doing so. And whether you like it or not, this nation would have suffered much more trouble had it not gone to liberate others. Even if it was a fiasco, I examine the hearts, and you are not judge. I examine the hearts, not you.

Hear what I Am saying, O My people, who call yourselves by My name. I hate no one. I hate only sin. I Am against no one, I Am against sin. If you are committing it, then I Am against you unless you repent. When you break from Mine anointed and you think I Am with you, it is described completely what I think about it in Psalm 2. Don't be mistaken, the vessel's hand I Am using is not saying this. These words are in My Word, and its name is the Bible. And she is only typing what it says.

Some of My prophets who call themselves by My name are a disappointment to Me, for they do not know Me as they claim. Not all of them, but those who are shallow and think they are something. They support those who are capable of wicked things all because they look like they could be Mine, or they act like they could be Mine; they even are relaxed and smile like they could be Mine. I assure you, no one is Mine who can destroy the innocent. Not that I hate them but that I simply Am not with their wicked works, and their success comes from those who support things that are not of Me. And that success and support will surely destroy them in the end if they do not repent.

We will go back in time, and I will describe My first visit to her. Many years ago when she was very young as a Christian, she was home all alone. She lived farther out in the country, and her husband was not home. It was about three o'clock in the morning, and someone knocked at the door. By this time in her life, Satan had bombarded her repeatedly, and she knew when an evil spirit was present. She knew so little about how to protect herself from Satan, and I wanted to reveal to her My Power and Presence in such a real way that there would be no doubt as to Who I Am. A young man appeared out of nowhere and asked if he could come in and use the telephone. She answered no, and as she turned away from the door, she felt an evil presence sweep through the room from him. To her, it was the most powerful presence of that kind that she had ever felt before; and before she could become frightened, I immediately stood before her as an angel. And all that had tried to enter her home in one moment had disappeared. I spoke, 'You think that is powerful, then feel this!' She was so small before Me, and she immediately fell to her knees, and she bent over with her head buried in her lap. She had her eyes covered with her arms, and even though her head was buried, she could still see Me plainly as though she was still looking up. With her eyes still closed, she could see the sword in My hand as I raised it above her. In seeing all this above her, she knew she was powerless to move or think to prevent Me. And I swung My sword full force through her body, and she could feel what it felt like to die physically without being dead and what it felt like to die spiritually without being dead, and she trembled. When I say what it felt like to be dead spiritually, I am speaking about the way Ananias and Sapphira felt when they fell over dead for lying to the Holy Spirit in the book of Acts chapter 5. They were consumed by My Consuming Fire. And for one moment, she knew exactly how they felt. As she trembled and a few seconds passed, she was about to look up when once again I swung My sword, and she felt exactly the same thing from the other direction as I backhanded this swing. She felt what it was like to die physically and what it was like to die spiritually. It took her a few seconds before she realized that she wasn't dead. And as I stood before her, she asked me the same question each time I visited her, which was a couple of weeks ago. And that question was 'Why am I not dead?' and My words to her were 'Because you belong to Jesus Christ.' I spoke to her plainly and simply and gave her the understanding that every church that belongs to Jesus Christ has an angel to protect it. They stand at the church to cut down anyone who comes against the Holy Spirit within the church to harm the church.

My main purpose for the whole visit was to reveal to her not to ever be afraid of anyone or anything that comes from people or from Satan. And from that day on, she obeyed Me. She had become afraid of no one except Me the Lord. She went and did all that I asked her to do and still does without any fear of any man or anything but I the Lord. Please do not puff yourselves up as to believe that I would destroy anyone that touches you during the time that you play your games with Me. Please do not think for one moment that you are able to send destroying angels. All too often those that claim to be Mine, which claim that I will take care of their enemies, cannot see that all along what they have been doing is as bad as their enemies. I said I stand at the church, I defend it, and I will destroy the enemies of the Holy Spirit. Many of you who claim My name are still My enemy, and your church is not defended by Me. I will defend every church of Mine from being destroyed. If your church is destroyed, ask yourself a question, where is your disobedience? Search that out so you will be able to repent.

I Am faithful in My Presence to every church. Not because the pastor is anything and not because the people are anything, but because I Am God and I promised in My Word that I would be faithful.

In order to deliver this message, My prophet had to endure my terror repeatedly. She would lie before Me for hours. Suspended in My time, which is the here and the now, where there is no tomorrow, no yesterday, only now. To her, she was not on the floor; she was somewhere in time. Because I called her out of time and all around her was nothingness. All she felt or knew was a tremendous awareness of right now that I the Lord was deciding if I was going to cast her away from My Presence *forever*.

Now, listen to what I Am saying here. I did not say that I was considering casting her away. I said that she felt as though I was considering casting her away. And I let her think that so that she would know what it felt like, so that she could come out of it and tell it to warn those who do not believe 'that it is a fearful thing to fall into the hands of the Living God' as written in Hebrews 10:13 (KJV). I have given the experience of visiting hell to some to have them come back and tell it. I have given them the experience to visit heaven to come back and tell it. This one I have visited with My glory that she may tell it.

She laid in My Presence for hours, and My Presence touched every atom of her being. She was unable to form one thought. All she had was a total awareness of the presence of My Spirit and of My being on the verge of making a decision concerning her soul. She could feel the 'now' of it, that in one second, in one moment, a decision was being made for all eternity concerning not only her life but also her spirit. And she was powerless to lift one finger or say one word, to do one thing to affect or change My decision. There was no defense, no excuse that could come to mind. No remembrance of knowledge of anything that she had ever said or done, for that was past and this is the now. The only way that it could be explained to you, and it is not her explanation, is when you meet Me, there is no such thing as remembering anything to utter an excuse because I hold all the memories; I hold all of the things needed for that decision in that day, not you. My, how you have puffed yourselves up to actually believe that you will be able to speak or remember in My Presence. Your choices and abilities end here when it comes to excuses. For in rejecting the truth, there are no excuses.

I describe it plainly in Psalm 1 that the *ungodly will not stand at the judgment.* The ungodly are not like the sinner who knows nothing. They are opposite of godly because they know better and refuse to repent. This is why it is very important to read the Bible to be able to see yourselves as I see you, not as you gloss over anything to be. Yes, it is very much like a courtroom. And yes, the books will be opened. But while they are opening, you will not have the opportunity to plead your case. Here on earth, an evil lawyer can plead a case for a reasonable doubt. But up here with Me, there is no such thing as being able to prove or plead a reasonable doubt for some of you. Your case is being pled *here and now* as you *reason with Me, in prayer.* And since you have been given every chance here and did not use it, in eternity you have just run out of chances. Read My Word. If any man tells you differently and you choose to believe what they have taught you and not what I taught in

11

My Word, that was simply your choice. All choices have consequences, some to the good and some to the bad.

Terrorized by My Presence so completely, she waited and waited, or it would be better for you to know that she endured and endured and endured. She could actually feel that she would be gone forever in one second, unable to ever change the decision forming in My mind. When I finally released her, she asked Me why she went through that. And I gave her a word of knowledge, and I said 'passion.' Her passion for Me burned so hot that she was willing to endure anything, suffer anything if only she could please Me. She went through the stages of thinking that she could please Me with all the things that she did for Me or the church. She discovered that there was only one way to please Me, and it is written in Hebrews chapter 11. This was all she ever desired, and this was My will. This was only one touch of My Spirit and My glory. And it was done to make it real not only to her but also to you that I Am the Lord and there is no other. To make it so real that I do cast souls into outer darkness, away from My Presence. That I do make decisions as to what I am going to do and no one, I repeat, no one will be able to say one word, give one excuse. In that day, I will do according to every man's works in Me.

You say you did not know, nor did you understand. Well, now is the time to say that to Me. Now is the time that you can plead your case. But I assure you, I will say to you as written in Peter that there are those who make themselves *willingly ignorant* of one great *fact. That the world was formed by the Word* and that the Bible sat in your home or your parents' home all of your life, and never did you ever decide to sit down and read it. Your whole life passed by, and you refused to read about My Son and what *He* said. Oh, I know you went to church faithfully. But you do not find salvation in Jesus Christ in a church that teaches another gospel and tells you that if you do not obey the church leaders, you are not getting into heaven when they themselves won't obey the only leader; and that is Jesus Christ, *Who is the Word.* Read it in the gospel of John chapter 1, verse 1. You never searched the scriptures to find Me.

Try as you might, you cannot get up above Me, nor can you get around Me. The belief that you will be able to stand before Me and that there will be one reason that you will be able to cause Me to change My mind where you will spend eternity is in error. For some in that day at the Judgment, the judgment will already be done; all that will be left is the sentence. No chance of deliverance then, no chance of turning away from it then, and no opportunity to make any choice then. Revelation 22:10-12 (KJV) says, 'And he saith unto me, Seal not the sayings of the prophecy of this book: for the time is at hand. He that is unjust, let him be unjust still: and he which is filthy, let him be filthy still: and he that is righteous, let him be righteous still: and he that is holy, let him be holy still. And, behold, I come quickly; and my reward is with Me, to give every man according as his work shall be.' Whatever state you meet Me in is the state of being you will remain throughout all eternity. The line gets drawn, no more chances.

I did make a decision that very day. I decided how I was going to eventually use her. During that time, she had a tumor below her left breast; and she was exhausted from the experience, so much so that she fell fast asleep. As she slept, I put My hand inside of her and held the tumor in my hand and squeezed it. I dissolved it the way I put My hand in Adam's body as he slept and took out his rib to make Eve. In her sleep, she felt the pain of My hand crushing it; and when she woke up, it was completely gone. She never asked Me to heal it, just like she never asked Me to heal her of cancer. All she ever wanted was to be with Me. That is love, and even I marveled at it. This is what I hope through this book to spring forth in you. She cried constantly to do My will, even if she had to die, and many times she almost did. Her spirit during that time would just slip away, and with My hand I held it within her body. Sometimes her body was so weak that her heart could not take the strain, and she would just slip away ever so softly, and I ever so gently held her within My great hand.

If only you could find it in your heart to be like Jesus in her and take your hands off the controls of your life and die daily. Because tears endure for a night but joy does come in the morning. That light that was to shine in you, you being the person reading this book, that light was ever so slowly snuffed out. Lying to yourself took you to only one place, one course, one road: repentance. What you never truly did the first time, no matter who you know or where you go, until you help Me to do the first works and bring Me meat worthy of repentance, you will remain self-deceived until it is too late. Because you have known I was there from the time you were little doesn't mean that you did what I wanted you to do within My Word. It only means that I called you, and you went your own way in religion, not in My Word. Because you had some knowledge of Me and My Word for years ahead of those that you do know means nothing to Me. It is what you did with it, not by making excuses that you do not act according to the Word because God is still working on you. The true answer is to back up and admit you are wrong and that you are like everyone else, you have to get on your knees and ask for forgiveness and to be led to repentance. What a silly person you are to think that I Am with you when you dare speak constantly that you know, you know, and you never humble yourself before Me in someone who does behave themselves properly. How long do I have to suffer your years of claiming that you are Mine and you know, but you have no true humility? Accountability, responsibility, and much more get thrown out the window when you see yourself as perfect before you permit Me through the Word to perfect you.

This is why for *this* time, for *this* hour, My hand is writing *this* book in the hopes that there will be some of you who will be willing to see yourself as you really are. No matter how high you sit, no matter how long you have sat there, no matter how many people supposedly love and respect you, no matter how much you believe or think you have, you need to examine yourself *today*. *For today is the day of salvation.* This is the now. Look around you. Is there any place that is a promised security in life that you will not have to face Me and soon? I say look around you because if you do, you will see that no one has any guarantee of a tomorrow, not even *as you know it* (meaning your quality of life financially and physically) not being taken away from you.

A short while ago, I came to her again. She did something that all of you take so lightly; therefore, I will not tell you what it is, lest you judge her. Right in the middle of it, My Glory appeared, and she knew

14

that any second she could be gone forever. I told her, 'Do you not know that right now, at this exact moment, I could take you out and cast you away from My presence for all eternity?' She was getting into the vehicle with her husband at the time, and she turned to look at him to see if he could feel what she felt. And I said, 'I could make it look like a heart attack or anything that I so desire, but believe Me, I will take you if you continue.' This was the harshest that I have ever been to her, and she cried out because of the reality of Who I Am. I was so real to her that she could not bring herself to want to breathe for the next couple of seconds. She could see clearly that she could not live without My Presence so much that she was like a baby feeling for every step in every second of her life. Get this picture in your mind: what she could not bear was her knowing that she would be without My Spirit, My Presence for even a moment, let alone facing that reality for eternity. Crying out to Me, she did not want to live any longer if she would repeat the same mistake and come to this very same place. She begged Me to take her life. And I settled her down and gave her the blessing of My Spirit, and she once again basked in My Presence and was comforted by Me and Me alone. Do the words like 'castaway' or 'outer darkness' mean anything to you? Does that ring a bell? Perhaps as we continue, it will occur to some of you how important it is not to leave a calling that I have called you to and place yourself where you don't belong.

Please, for your sake, don't be deceived into believing that she sinned so badly that I dealt with her so harshly, because *the only reason she endured these things was to tell it.* I wanted to make it real to *you* through her testimony that *I Am God.* In Luke 13:2-5 (KJV) it says, 'And Jesus answering said unto them, Suppose ye that these Galileans were sinners above all the Galileans, because they suffered such things? I tell you, Nay; but except ye repent ye shall likewise perish. Or those eighteen, upon whom the tower of Siloam fell, and slew them, think ye that they were sinners above all men that dwelt in Jerusalem? I tell you, nay; but, except ye repent, ye shall all likewise perish.' I spoke in Isaiah 43 (KJV) that I called you to be My witnesses that *I Am God.*

When I healed her, I put a song within her, to make it real, to tell how I saw the whole situation, to tell what I wanted her to see, that

15

she may be able to tell it to you. 'Mine eyes have seen the glory of the coming of the Lord; *He hath trampled out the vintage where the grapes of wrath are stored. He hath loosed the faithful lightening of His terrible swift sword; His truth is marching on, glory, glory Halleluiah, glory, glory, Halleluiah.'* Can you see it? Can you see what I am saying to you? The lightning of the Word of God penetrated within her down to the bone and the marrow of her heart; that is where the grapes of wrath are stored in the heart. God hates the sin that is cultivated by the heart to say that makes all of His commandments vain. He trampled them out with His faithful *terrible swift* sword. For in the moment that I came in My Glory, I revealed to her, her sin against the Word. Listen please, I appeal to you, it is real.

If you think for one moment in anything that you have read that you would have done a better job than her, or would not have done the things she did, I am telling you the truth, repent, because you are the one who is so much worse off than she has ever been. Listen carefully and get it right down into your ears. *Her eyes have seen the glory of the coming of the Lord.* I Am going to visit everyone who claims to be Mine in this manner. If they are where they ought to be, then they will be filled with joy and blessing; but if they are self-deceived, they can and will wish that they never forced My hand within them. Listen to what I say. *Within them, the Holy Spirit within you.* I will touch you, and it will not be a blessing to your flesh if you lie to me. If you continue in your farce of claiming I Am with you or called you to be something that I never called you to, you will know in that day that I Am God! But I Am merciful also and will give you the opportunity to repent before I come. So do it now, for *today is the day of salvation.*

And if you turn this in your head and your heart to say this cannot be God, for it is threatening, remember this one thing. If this is a man's message, it would be a threat. But since it is directly from Me, it is a warning. A warning that is designed to lead you to repentance and to ask for forgiveness and work it all out with Me. Psalm 51:4 (KJV) says, 'Against Thee, Thee, only, have I sinned, and done this evil in Thy sight: that Thou mightest be justified when Thou speakest, and be clear when Thou judgest.' This vessel has nothing to do with what I Am saying; as a matter of fact, she would never write a single word unless she knows that I said those words.

The last visit was not that difficult for her to endure. She could feel in My Spirit that it was I, and she could feel My terrorizing presence, but she could also feel that it felt good to her. Because now she was so close to Me that when I come and visit, the flesh isn't reigning and is not in control enough to be terrorized. The Spirit rules and reigns completely, and we have sweet fellowship together, and I use this Presence as a way to let her know that I Am the same God Who has power over life and death, over heaven and hell, over all that she is and all that she will be, and she has a peace that was borne out of the most comforting love that any person could have with an awesome God. Many times as she was writing, doubt would come to her, was she to really write this? And I would allow her to feel My terrorizing presence, not harshly but enough that I could speak through My glory as a reminder and ask her this gently, 'How could you doubt?'

After the first visit where she lay for hours, she then begged Me over and over and over to never touch her again like that. Then as she grew in Me, she began to realize what that visit did; it changed something within her. She realized how it changed her and gave her the power to do and overcome things that she took so lightly before. And she began to pray for Me to come again just like that and help her to be where she needs to be. Knowing how traumatic it was for her in the physical sense, she still desired to be close to Me, and I answered her cry. Now, no longer does she beg Me to not come to her that way. She prays, 'If I need it, I need it, please come, Lord.'

Last year, she laid her head on the bed to retire for the night. Suddenly My terrorizing presence came right out from within her being. This Presence she knows so well. The Presence of My Glory came right out of her heart. I intensified quickly and immediately; and by the time she could ask Me what was going on, why did she experience this, I said, 'I wanted you to know the power within you.' I revealed to her that the power within her was equal to the power that the apostles had when Ananias and Sapphira lied to the Holy Spirit within them and paid for it. Are you lying to Me and thinking all is well with your soul? Make it

17

right today, now. For today is the day of salvation. There is nothing that is able to separate you from My love. Romans 8:38, 39 (KJV) says, 'For I am persuaded that neither death nor life, nor angels, nor principalities, nor powers, nor things present, nor things to come. Nor height nor depth, nor any other creature shall be able to separate us from the love that is in Christ Jesus our Lord.' No angel can separate you, no one can separate you. *The only person who can is you.* By choice, by rejection of the truth or reception of the lie because only the truth will set you free. Every soul that has My Holy Spirit indwelling and every day of their lives they reject Me and cause Me to dwell where they take Me. And they do this *without the fear of Me* that they need to benefit their soul.

Many of you thus far have taken all this so lightly. It is a very important hour upon the church right now, and the only way you are safe is to be safe in the arms of Jesus through the power of His Word guided by My Holy Spirit. Dangerous times are coming. Some of you believe that those times that are to come will be seen by the flesh of perhaps losing what you financially have, perhaps someone invading your life, because as always your thinking is geared toward everything and anything of the flesh, and very little of the Spirit is ever seen. As you protect one door, another tries to open; and you must, more than ever before, run to the Only One who loves you. But another danger lurks, and you may not believe what is about to be written, and I am going to reveal the truth in My Word, why it is so important to know how to possess your vessel and how to make sure you are obeying the Word. Because surely in an hour you think not the Son will come and He will bring His reward with Him. And for those of you who value Him in your soul, it will be a day of complete joy that no man can take away. And to ensure that moment, take heed to what is written.

While it is true that you need to develop an attitude, you must desire the best attitude, because if that attitude is not to die for Me to live in you, then what can you accomplish for Me? Your attitude can accomplish much for you, but very little for Me. The attitude of the vessel who is writing this book has always been that of 'If I die, I die, but I will not glorify the enemy and go down in believing that I have no power to overcome. If God doesn't save me, then if I perish, so I perish.

But I will not relinquish my belief that God loves me and desires the best for me. If I'm poor, I'm poor, but I will always believe that God desired more for me.'

Every step, every thought that this vessel took was always giving Me all the glory. That attitude holds a lot of weight with Me. Without a heart that has been completely cleansed by the blood of Jesus, without a mind that has completely led every thought captive to Christ through the Word and the presence of the Holy Spirit, all through obedience to the Word and allowing Jesus Christ to take up an abiding residence in you, it is impossible to accomplish. You will always find yourself enduring temptation to the flesh when it can be overcome in the Word. Get the attitude that is willing to go through anything, endure anything to obey Me in the Word; and by your faith in the Word, I will honor you as I have honored her. All of My prophets must have this attitude, for this attitude leaves no place for the flesh, the world or the devil. 'Thy will be done, not mine but Thine.' That is the attitude of Jesus Christ."

PART II

"And Jesus knew their thoughts, and said unto them, every kingdom divided against itself is brought to desolation; and every city or house divided against itself shall not stand" (Matthew 12:25 KJV).

What you are about to read about this nation is not to find fault with it. Not to find fault with those who are My people. This nation is the greatest and will continue to be the greatest country in the world if its people stop allowing corruption to take place beginning with the so-called church. None of it is written to cause you to give up desiring to see someone who is in your ethnic group or gender succeed in anything that they put their hands to in this great nation. The American dream that everyone speaks about or thinks about is only obtainable by My grace. I cause it to rain on the just and unjust alike. Success never means that you are right, that you are pleasing to Me, nor does it mean that it is My will. But many of you apply those thoughts and principles to what you think is Me. It is because so many are very mistaken, and in such a perilous condition of their soul that I state these things clearly and precisely out of My great love for My people.

If I called a president and he made any mistakes while he needed your support and not your criticism, when he needed you to decide to

20

do what I called you to do, to care for others more than yourself, to pray for your leaders and not according to biased news media. And you destroyed him by simply turning your back on him and your heart says, "I won't touch this, let him hang himself." Setting traps for him from ignorant nations and people is one thing, but those of you who attend church as Christians? Haven't you noticed that never once has he opened his mouth against anybody? Yes, he stands for what he believes is right and speaks it but never to devour you and destroy you; I have not seen it yet. And if anybody should be doing this, it should be him. And the media and some of you have seen his strength that comes from Me as a weakness. I laugh at that because none of you could handle what he has had to handle, that is why I put him there even though some of you are so foolish that you believe he stole it from you. Mistakes or no mistakes, he is Mine. I Am not ashamed of him because he is not ashamed of Me.

I know that there will be those of you who will twist and turn these words to suit yourselves and make this all appear to your own advantage. You are the same people that twisted and turned My Words in the Bible, so why would you be different now? The warnings here are to remind you that when you do, it is not for your good or for your spiritual good but in direct opposition to your own souls. I will not marvel at your ability to destroy yourself after all of you read the Bible or you heard it preached and made a decision to twist and turn it all up to enable you to do evil.

From beginning to end of this book, I have but one desire, and that is to help *anyone* who wants to be able to see themselves the way I see them, that they may change their attitude toward Me, their feelings toward Me, and change their ways. Many of you are driven by your emotions; you are controlled by them. The thoughts of consequences concerning your decisions never come, and most of the time fear is your main driving factor. You desire change, and as much as you desire a change for your life, as God, so do I. For I love you. But I will always honor My Word. And you will not always like that. And when you are in opposition to it, then *you are in opposition to yourself.* For no choice ever hurts or disturbs Me and My purpose. It can and will only destroy you, and because of that, I write this book. I have a continuous unconditional love that continually strives to change your mind and your heart until the day that it is all too late.

In this nation, I have many great prophets. They are those who teach and preach about prophetic revelation through dreams and visions. Not your secular inward soulish teachings but those that reveal how God interprets and teaches. There are those who teach you how to possess your vessel, how to be what I called you to be. Many of Mine I Am well pleased with. Some with great wisdom and understanding, some with tremendous gifts of healings, and one great one that preaches and teaches every aspect of the gospel from the beginning of My Word to the end. Some are great ones who warn everyone about the nation's leader and other nations. These men and women are great in Me, and I love their work, and I claim them as Mine. And there are those who go out to other countries. But I must warn those from other countries, I do not call anyone outside of this country to prophesy over anything in this country. I call each one to his own place.

Stay where you are called. You enter in and touch when you have no idea of what is really going on, and you make yourself look great to many, but I Am not well pleased.

This nation is divided against itself and has been for a long time. When I say this, I Am not speaking about the part of the nation that doesn't know Me, doesn't want Me, and defies Me. I Am speaking to the ones *who claim to know Me* through the Word and claim to have My Holy Spirit. Those of you who attend church also have done so much to cause this nation to be practically split right down the middle. All of you who call yourself by My name see it and know it. This isn't any great secret. The secret is that many of you have simply given up and quit believing the Word. Because of so many things that seem to have come to pass, you are greatly discouraged even though you have taken a firm stand against the destruction of innocent lives. So much so that you *let* things come about in your lives that you have power over. In this day more than ever before, each person has their own agenda, and each one sides with brother against brother. A brother has the attitude that he can say or do anything because he is a brother but don't dare let anyone do or say the same things to his brothers. That is the attitude of a sibling when they are little; some people never grow up, because it is carried into adulthood and into the church. I say that you should never think or believe that it is all right for you to call your brothers names; it is not all right if you speak about them with disrespect, for they are your brothers. But you say that if another speaks it, it is wrong. I say if *you speak any evil name-calling, it is wrong.* This has been going on for a long time. And many of you have the attitude that these things have always been and always will be. I Am not speaking of the world, nor Am I speaking of the worldly church that is filled with those who follow after the teachings and doctrines of men, traditions that go against My Word. Those who have made a decision to hang on to what someone else has told them rather than follow My Word, they will have no real part in Me unless they repent. Rather, I Am speaking to those who know the Word and claim to have My Holy Spirit.

Satan has a plan, one that he wants you to fall head-on into. That plan is to use you to destroy your brother in Christ and use him to destroy you. One of the worst ways of doing this is the pointing of the finger spoken about in Isaiah. As long as you call the mistakes or sins of others to attention, you think that no one can see what you are doing. And you hide behind what you say about them, but I see you, I hear you, and when that time comes, you will know that you never deceived Me, that you never distracted Me from the truth. Remember what makes manifest is light, and no one will escape the light.

These are divided against themselves when it comes to this nation. You don't think so? See, even now, even your most famous prophets support one against another, forgetting what My Word says. Yes, you should support a leader once I put him or her in office, but you should never speak *for* any man except to say that you believe that *I* called him or her for this hour in this nation, and after they take office, *you* then need to support them in prayer. But if this nation falls to such a point that an *ungodly* person takes office that believes it is all right to kill the innocent, and I am speaking of babies, that they can see their grandchildren destroyed because they view the baby as a punishment to their children who perhaps made a mistake, do not support them in your prayers, for you are asking Me to be partaker of evil, and I will not. If a man does wrong and associates with the wrong people, he should be man enough to realize that he has a consequence to face. He should own up to his wrongs, not twist and turn them and lie about them. When you do wrong and say wrong and then say you did not mean that or that it was taken out of context, a lie is a lie is a lie. No lie will enter heaven, also nothing that makes a lie. I know your heart, and you answer to Me; although you continue just because you have the power to make yourself sound so good, that does not mean that it is all right with Me.

Movie stars sound good, and some of them are worshipped; singers sound good, and some of them are worshipped. Silly *little* girls think they are so sexy. Silly people are their following. Women past the age of thinking such silliness speak of some men being sexy. I Am not against anyone because they are of a certain race, ethnic background, or gender. What I Am against is when that person does things or says things and claims that I Am with them. *Have you not read that you will be judged by your words and by those words you will either stand or fall? To the point that even now what you have said in the past comes out into the open because I put it forth into the light.* Here on earth, men will try to hold you to your words, and it will seem like you slipped out with My help. I tell you now, I did not help you because according to My Word you need to make things right. When any one of you do things and say things that are not of Me and then you say that you did not say them or they are taken out of context, tell Me, how can I be with you when I do not change, nor do I ever lie? I Am speaking to all. I made up My mind that I would reveal what is very important to Me, and I would never tell anyone that it is unimportant if you have said or done things that you have not made right; lying about them or denying them is not making them right. Whatever makes manifest is the light. Whatever you hear in the ear, My Word tells you to cause it to be shouted upon the housetops.

Walk honestly. This is all I desire out of My people: to walk honestly and with integrity. Stick to not doing these things instead of lying and saying they were never said, never done, never intended, or taken out of context. This is not to say that I find such fault with you that I will refuse you if you repent. I wait for that. But when people make their mistakes out in the open where millions of people can see them, how can you believe that I will not correct you if you claim that you belong to Me? I want no parts of anyone believing that I Am speaking about this because I want or don't want someone in public life to succeed.

You say on one hand this is unfair, for your ability to have power is hanging in the balance. I say if you are not ready for it, you are not ready for it. And when the time comes that *you strive to obtain it through good and not evil, you then may have it.* When the end, if whatever you strive to accomplish is evil, remember that end achievement doesn't justify the means. *When the means are good overcoming evil, then I can hear your voice.* But how can I hear the voice of hatred? How can I hear the voice of slipping and sliding in and out of things? Tell Me, where did you ever get the impression that people are so blind they cannot see the truth through all the lies; worse yet, where did you ever get the idea that it somehow is all going to be all right with Me? There are those who are more than willing to see your group or gender in office that are righteous and holy, but they can see the truth, and in their conscience, they cannot support a lie. And *you will have done it, and you will lose even though you will blame everyone else.* In that day, you will never be able to say to Me that someone stole it from you. When will some of you grow up and accept responsibility for your own actions? Instead of blaming your failures on your plight in life on everyone else, when will the day come that you will say I could have done better and strive to do so? I said you can do all things in Jesus Christ who strengthens you, but I never said that you can do all things that go against My Word and still be in Jesus.

Those of you who claim to be Mine and have weighed this out and are sure that to get someone to obtain what you desire for those you have a passion for, those that you desire to get ahead, remember that I send strong delusion that you may believe a lie. Take a good look at what and who is on the scene. I promise you in the end, you will find out it is not Me. In Jesus there is no darkness *at all.* And if you have weighed it out and thought for one moment that I weigh it with your balance, I Am warning you even now this is not so. You must weigh things with a righteous balance in obedience to My Word. You say that is impossible in this day and age that you now live in. I tell you that I *never* change no matter what day and age you live in. You are empowering the wrong person. You want to see an American tragedy, then continue to support anyone who can destroy children because if they can do that, they can do anything. And although I love all of you, although I desire all of you to get ahead, I will not ever change My Word because you cried.

Every person who claims Jesus Christ has a certain amount of righteousness within Him even those with the most limited amount of knowledge of the Word. But not every man lives what he *claims to believe. From the worldliest person to the godliest, those portions of the Word can be seen if they ever had anything to do with Jesus' Word. I wrote clearly in My Word that you will know them by their fruits. It is not the amount of people that they are able to persuade.* Not the amount of people that they are able to take on an emotional roller-coaster ride anytime they make fair speeches. *It is not the amount of people that they are not able to persuade. By their fruits, you shall know them. You must ask yourself, do the people that I am tempted to support think it is all right to destroy or kill a helpless life within a woman's body? Do you honestly believe that I would take part in such a thing, to being as evil as a man or a woman who would willfully and deliberately destroy the helpless individual living within a woman? All that I created, all that I put into the intricate miracle of birth. How impossible it is for anyone to become pregnant except by miracle, and I would give permission to willfully and deliberately kill it as though it was not made in My image. Because you still don't get it. I choose who is born and who is not. Read Romans, what happens when you take the image of the Creator and turn it into the image of the creature which is man. When you tell a woman she has a right to choose to destroy her child, right there you changed My image to be like yours. You then made yourself God.*

Because a man or a woman or any ethnic group or a particular gender group knows how to answer and talk the talk doesn't mean that this is what I want. A person's fruits are evident by those whom he associates with. They are evident by the people he is in agreement with. These are the kind of people that you gather to yourself. If you are a gossipmonger, those who gossip will come running to you with every evil story. If you are a liar, all liars will love and support you. If you are a thief, thieves will be with you. If you love Me above all, I will draw all men unto Me. If you preach and teach to obey one of the least of My commandments, I will draw great men and women of God to you. Just because you now are in the public eye, you are able to say, pretend, or deny that you did anything against My word. Is this what I Am about? How do the two mix together? Oh, you were younger and made mistakes. All of you do, and that is a fact, for all have sinned and come short of the glory of God. It is one thing to do it, and it is still another to deny it or pretend you never did it. *Then*, your motives *should* be brought into question. Man won't bring them into question; *I will*.

Remember the world loves its own. This is the way that you can clearly see your source of power because I Am not of this world. When you see crowds from other nations loving a person, remember that the world loves its own. This may seem right to you, but there are not that many people who truly love the Lord. My Word clearly tells you that there are people who will honor one another and not honor those who love God. *My people need to remember I Am not looking for someone who is approved by the world, but rather someone who is approved by Me because they obey My Word. If you choose these people, they may succeed with your help. But I tell you even now, it is not My will, it is yours, so where do you think the blame will fall? What do you think will take place if I Am not with you?*

My church needs to be wise in their decisions of choices in life. I have said clearly in Romans chapter 13 that when you do right, you will have praise from authority; and if you don't, then you need to be afraid. If you have done anything that you should not have done and think you can just sweep it under the rug without repentance, you are wrong. I respond to honesty. Not to the person who says they know the people want them to be honest, but they in their doings are not. But *all* of you live your lives as though I do not exist. And the shock of it all is you claim the highest in the churches. This nation is polarized by two extremes. You can see the extremes in the world clearly, but do you have enough wisdom to see them spiritually? On the one side, there are those who have the Word, or at least some knowledge of it. They want no parts of the Holy Spirit; they deny that God does anything today, that all of it was in the past, that God today is dead, no longer powerful enough to do what He used to do through His children. They do things their way all the while they claim Me. On the other side, you have those who know the Holy Spirit is in operation today as He was then, yet they never get into the Word because they love Me; they only get into it to *obtain* their needs or wants. Try to bring the two together and it is like the pull of two equally powerful magnets face-to-face, they will repel each other. When they are in opposition, they repel; but if they got on board and got together and worked alongside, then they would not repel each other. One side would have to accept the Holy Spirit as written in the book of Acts, and the other would have to get completely into the Word. But this can never be in the present state both are in. They will never come together with the magnetic power equal on both sides. By your own lives and actions, you prove to Me daily that you want no parts of My Word. And they want no part of My Spirit. Oh, I know, you say that's not so. Ask yourself how many times do you pick up the Word and read it, let alone ponder it and meditate on it. Ask yourself how many times you did this *just to know Me and understand Me.* Not how many times you picked it up to save yourself from circumstances, situations, afflictions, financial crisis, etc. How many times do you pick it up just to get to know My Son that died for you? Both sides claim Me, both sides reject Me. You don't think so. Read on and you will see.

On the other side, you have all your traditions that you think you are following according to Me. You have a form or a formula you operate in. You made the decision that I Am not the same today as I was yesterday, and because of that you became entangled in things of no importance, things that don't mean anything. Your refusal to believe that the Holy Spirit is given to you at conversion, giving you the power to seek Me in My Word that I may lead you into the truth. The book of Acts was written for all to realize that what I did then, I do now, how I worked with people I work now. But no, *you chose to deny Me; therefore, you deny yourself the benefits of everything that I left for you. And why are you so deluded, because you received not the love of the truth.*

Today there are many people that are bipolar. They act exactly like the condition of the nation and the so-called Christian church. Their emotions and minds go from one extreme to the other. In one moment they could love you so much they could die for you; do something to cross them and they can turn on you enough to destroy you. Watch the media, they do almost the same thing. They swing back and forth, watch almost everything in life, they swing back and forth. People are so fickle that one day they support this one, and one day they support that one. Why? I ask you why? Because you receive not the love of the truth, and you need to get on your knees and seek me until you find Me in the Word.

They talk about being bipolar as though they are mood swings. You have to be in the place that you do not follow Me in order to receive this. Do you know how many of these claim to be Christian? In your emotions on one hand you are flying high, and in a moment you can fall into the deepest depression that only God can pull you out of. Why do you think all these things come upon you? *It is because there is no Word within your heart and mind? Worse yet, you say you have the Word, you say you belong to Jesus, you say that you go to church, you think you are where you need to be.* Your loving Me enough to seek Me in the word has been denied and traded for instant satisfaction. I want what I want right now, which is the attitude, and with it, you get what you don't want right now, and you wonder why.

Many of My people in this nation claim Me and do not go to church. Church to them means involvement in their lives, and they have been there and have done that until they got burnt out by someone who never preached or told them that their first duty was to their own families. They deserted their families and lost them, or they fought to get them into their church when they clearly did not know what they were talking about. Silence in patience and learning would have worked better even if it took years. Perhaps someone hurt their feelings or did something against them. Perhaps they saw someone in the church sinning, forgetting that all of you are only human. Or they can't control the preacher or control anybody; therefore, they go on to look for someone that their evil can control. You all want the signs and wonders.

29

You all want to be seen and noticed and even heard when you have nothing to say. *If it isn't the Holy Spirit speaking through the power of the Word in you, then what importance have you to Me?* They do not realize that they will never have *any* excuse for forsaking the assembling of themselves together. The bottom line is, they do not want to love the brethren the way I commanded. They are all out for self. What I said in My Word will stand. I Am *no* respecter of persons. I do not change *any* part of My Word simply because you made a decision not to attend any church. You can tell your friends, you can tell your neighbors, you can tell anyone why you refuse to honor Me at the least one day a week, and you may convince yourself and someone else, but you will never have the opportunity to make any excuses to Me. If you love Me, *you will* keep My commandments. Ask yourself a question, are you going to be in heaven all alone the way you are now? Interaction is part of fellowship, part of responsibility. And that is what you hate the most, being held responsible for your actions, being seen for what and who you really are. So you hide out, and because I have not corrected you yet, you believe it will all be all right. You believe that you have a special dispensation in your mind, *not in My mind*. You believe that you are serving an understanding God you say, one that knows that you cannot obey. Don't you see how foolish that is? Of course I know that no man can obey without My Spirit. But never do I give excuses, nor did I pass out licenses to sin. Oh, I know, while you're here you think that you have a free pass; after all, Abraham is your father. Not so. You are responsible for your Christian brother. When you do not attend church, you can never hear or see their need. You can never be there for their encouragement or correction, exhortation, or edification that each one of you need.

The pulpit that I give every soul is never to be used to destroy another. It is to glorify My Son by lifting Him up enough that they will know you are Christians by your love. I am telling you plainly that no matter what condition of life you were born in, if you sincerely follow Me and My Word and pick up your cross and die daily to what you want or think, I can and I will change all of your life. Not that it will be a rose garden because I promised tribulation in the world, and I promised persecution. Do you honestly believe that I Am with anyone who disrespects even one person that I made in My image? My Word is clear that you are to respect *all* men. Not some. I never taught any of you to have respect for only those who are like you. I give you the right to defend your nation and your home. I Am with you when you do. But brother against brother is not of Me. Your brother is any color; *you are to be a Christian first.* And that doesn't mean to accept those who say they have the word and live like demons. I Am not telling you to accept a person because they are a certain color or to not accept them because they are not a certain color; what I Am telling you is this, color has nothing to do with it. All of you are brothers *if* you belong to Me. And if you belong to Me, you will know them by their fruits. And the fruits of Mine do not include destroying the innocent who are helpless to defend themselves. Nor does it include same-sex marriages and making provisions for them as though I would bless such a union. You call yourself Mine, then you had better be Mine and stand up against what is wrong. Yes, it is true that they have a right to their choice; and although I do not hate any of them and love every soul I created, I do not ever intend to be misunderstood that I would bless such a union. All of these things are something done against themselves. I do not lift a finger against them; they are against themselves when they disobey My Word. They have a right to visit each other in the hospitals, they have a right to choose a lot of things, but they have no right to expect the same blessings of a union between a man and a woman. When they make their commitments without Me, then they must realize they will suffer the consequences of their choices. It is not your job to even hate their sins, it is not your job to destroy them or hurt them or even deny them Christian love. It is your Christian responsibility to be there when they have important needs for prayer in the hopes that they will see that I love them and repent. It is up to you to help them realize the error of their ways without enticing hatred.

Oh, I see, the members of your own parties will crucify those who dare to believe that I hate these sins. They will twist and turn it to make it look like you are an extremist. Yet Jesus endured all of this, and if they

31

killed Him for telling the truth, they will try to destroy your power to speak it.

Now if I choose to bless you here or in heaven, that is something that you are entitled to in Christ but never to hurt another to get it. Remember Jezebel and Ahab, they took what they thought belonged to them also. She whispered a lie into his ear. Since he was a king, all he had to do was murder the real owner and take it. Have you not heard that it is wrong to covet what another has and claim that because you don't have it I would rob someone to give it to you? What is the matter with you? Because you are without gives, you no right to demand to have what belongs to another, what they labored for. If they applied themselves to educate themselves enough to earn something, why would I just give it to you? These are things that split this nation.

A house divided cannot stand. If you are not loyal to your own country, how can you ever be loyal to Me? If you are not loyal to your own family, how can you be loyal to Me? Those babies that are being destroyed are your children, your family, and in some case your grandchildren. How can you desire to destroy these by believing that it is a punishment to make a woman go through the pregnancy because you view a member of your family a punishment; therefore, they must be destroyed. Where, I ask you, is your mind? Listen, those of you who preach that I will give and give and give because you feel sorry for people who are struggling because of their need. You need to examine why you go against My Word. Because a person is in need and many times it is because they do not properly manage what they have, they do not even desire to find out how to change, and you tell them that they have something coming from Me if they believe My Word; you need to read again. I taught no such thing.

Justice is justice, right is right, doing things the right way, obtaining things the right way with hard work and determination, and developing the abilities and gifts that I gave you would bring prosperity to you. But it doesn't fall from heaven if you are not qualified. You say you are qualified by faith. Where have you ever gotten the impression that simply because you believe something it is My will or My way? You may seemingly have a power to operate and obtain, but I assure you it is not from Me.

It is time now to send the angels to separate the sheep from the goats. Those who are Mine will come with me in the "Rapture". Oh that's right. There is no such thing as the "rapture." No one is going to be left behind. All of you are Christians, and all of you are going up. You know the Word which is Jesus, that's all just symbolism, it's just a story, it doesn't mean a thing. Just keep on doing what you are doing; just keep on splitting your nation right in half. Right down the middle. There are more so-called reborn Christians in this nation than the few that show up when the time comes to vote. They have no interest in what happens to their nation, and they take interest only just before the time. Then they expect Me to tell them who to vote for. They don't do their homework of reading My Word that they may have discernment enough to recognize who is who, so they trust in the media to give them the truth, and as it is right now, they lie. They are of the world, and they will paint it all to make it look like they want. And you who claim to be Mine listen to them even when I reveal a clear difference; you permit them to use their words and ways to convince you that you need someone the world loves. You by reading filthy rags that call themselves news destroy My people, help destroy one who will live for me and stand up for My principles. You always forget that everyone is human and makes mistakes. But those who never turn from those mistakes are the ones you need to watch out for. Those who never admit their wrongs, never back up, and take humility as a weakness.

And there are those who use their churches to feed hatred, discord, etc. Fight and devour, and what will be your reward even if you seem to win? For what good will it do to gain the whole world and in the end lose your own soul? Continue to hate and be resentful; the only purpose that I intended for you to take a firm stand upon was My Word. Never did I intend for you to fight for a man or a woman to become something that they are not. Well, you're loyal in one place; and that is to your gladiators, your sports heroes, your movie stars. Very loyal to your rock stars and anyone else that you worship in My place. I have nothing against these things; what I hate is *you putting them in My place. Taking*

33

their word above Mine. The saddest part of all of this is how many of you claim to belong to My Son. The saddest thing is when you do not know, and it is all because you have not made it your business to know His Word.

I know that some of you are suffering and have been suffering, and it has been for generations. I know that you believe that I will deliver you from the people that you think are responsible for hurting you and your family for generations. Those generations were the *first* that you were to *forgive* and not carry it, teaching hatred to your children and your children's children, using it all for an excuse for permitting your lives to be wasted. And I know that you praise Me, and you wait on Me, and you expect that because you are poor and needy I will not forsake you and that I will lift My hand to deal with whom *you* believe is responsible. And when you think someone is against you that they will fall into their own self-made pits. And in some cases you actually believe that these people are going to hell. You ask Me for justice and judgment upon those whom you are convinced in your heart that they are responsible. You want these people put in fear; you want them to be held accountable. All as though you are perfect because you do praise Me, and you do witness on occasion and tell of My marvelous works. You also believe and give Me the glory by the fact that you know that had it not been for Me, you would have been dead long ago. All of these things *are not* enough to cause Me to bring judgment on any soul that you *think* has done you evil. You take My Word and apply it according to what you *think* destroyed your ancestors, destroyed all your chances of ever coming out of what has been done in the past and *none* of what you believe according to *your thinking* is true. Not that those you are against are innocent. But it is not up to you to make these judgments. And your leaders feed you this because they are in error. Some of you are innocent of this, but most are waiting for me to judge someone else. You do not realize the seriousness of the state that your soul is in. If and when I come to judge, I will judge *you first.*

Without ever obeying My Word by getting into it to know My Son, you have left the door open to bring judgment upon yourself with this attitude. I know, you're taught to take what is yours. There is nothing wrong with that teaching; it is true, there are things that are yours, they belong to you and Me. *But you have taken it upon yourself to believe what you believe, and you are striving to take what belongs to others.* And believing anything will never make it so, especially when it comes to these things. I did not lead you there in your thinking. Bitterness, resentment, envy, jealousy, greed, and many more led you into that belief. And when that bitterness rose up in *any* one of you, then many were defiled even to whole churches. You then become guilty of what you hate and claim that I desire to deliver you. And *I do indeed desire to deliver you.* True deliverance is *never* by the problem going away. It is *always* obtained in victory by *you,* retaining the truth of the Word within you no matter what your circumstances or condition. The truth that needs to be retained is that you do not curse those that you think destroyed your life. True deliverance is by being able to have the fruits of the Holy Spirit within you, and that cannot come about as long as you do not forgive one person or one offense. You are to forgive every ancestor, yours and theirs. Both are guilty because all are human. No matter how you paint it, no one is ever completely right on either side. The only One who is completely right is Jesus. As long as you hold on to the anger, resentment, and bitterness, you are not retaining the knowledge of Me which is manifested by the fruits that you bear. If your fruits are not unconditional love, then you do not have all the rest of them. You oppose yourselves and hinder your own soul and blame everyone else for the problem. And you need to repent. I cannot help you in this condition of life; My hands are tied by *you.*

If you want these things within your gender or your ethnic groups, then do things according to My Word and do them righteously, not with evil motivations that have such self-interests that you can think of yourself as some sort of savior. Many of you talk a lot about this nation needing to think of others and not themselves. But all you have on your mind is achieving what your agenda is. All you see is what you suffer and how badly you want delivered, and being a Christian is so much more than that.

You have gone so far that you believe that anybody that disagrees with you hates you or hates your gender or your group. Anybody who doesn't do what *you think* in your mind is *your enemy,* not Mine but yours; and you take it as though they hate you or your gender or your ethnic group. The way I Am describing it is the way it is *in* you. You believe you are humble because you are in need and you cry to Me and you turn My Word to work for you to apply it where and when *you want it* without ever truly seeking Me to apply it to *you enough* to be kind, gently forgiving, meek, long-suffering, peace, great peace to those who have it. The humble heart My Word speaks of is humble and contrite, which is *sorry for their* sin. Not always crying because they are in need, and most of the time they are in need because of their inability to overcome *their own* weaknesses. Or they are lusting for something and have no godly contentment and will never be satisfied.

There are those of you who do not understand the word "humility." Because you get on your knees and cry to Me because *you need*, because *you hurt*, that doesn't make you humble. If you were humbled, you would not dare come to Me as though I will destroy someone that *you think* is responsible for your condition of life. Many of you refuse to do the right thing with the life I gave you, and you refuse to find out how to do the right thing. Do you honestly believe that you have the power to persuade Me to send a soul to hell because *you* believe they are going there? All because they were not where you thought they ought to be or because they didn't do according to what you *think*. You think that they should do according to the things that are important *to you*. Am I supposed to work according to this all because of your condition, your circumstances? If you let all of life and all of your finances slip through your fingers, and then expect others to hand what they worked for to you, where Am I in this? I am not like you. You do not have control over Me. Oh, I see, you believe that I Am God and that I Am a rewarder of those who seek after Me diligently. And so I Am! And that somehow makes everything slanted on your side. You seek Me diligently *for your* need. Tell Me, how is selfishly, greedily taking My Word to your purpose seeking Me diligently? You take *part* of the Word and use it to work for you. *It is backward. You are supposed to work for Me. The Word is given for you to work for Me. Pick up your cross and deny yourself. How does that operate in your thinking?*

I Am not done with this president. Although you are playing the same old game, making him entirely to blame for what took place concerning anything in this country. *I freely gave My Son for you. Freely.* And many of you who are called by My name will not and have not *freely given yours for Me.* When I say for Me, I mean that I in My Word teach certain things that you have tossed out the window for your self-gratification. You ask Me how can I defend such a man. I can, I do, and I will. Before the whole world, they will see Me stand up and defend this nation. I cannot defend this nation without defending its leaders. If any are not worthy and many of them are not, then it is all in My hands, *not* yours. Ah, but then your pride is so great that you would never relinquish it all to Me, as though you have anything to do with it in your hands. Don't you realize that you delivered this president into the hands of your enemies and you listened to the call of the world and not of Me? And you are about to do the same things by listening to what the world wants, not what I want. The liberal media rips and tears and destroys, and you help them and spread the poison with your tongue. You read and enjoy all those filthy rags that call themselves a newspaper, exposing the truth. What do evil people know about truth? Tell Me, what does the destroyer that they are following, that you are following, know about truth? The truth is My Word. Stay on course with it and you will see who is who.

The self-seeking media, to make their living, run with any story; they reveal secrets that I never intended to be made known. They are irresponsible, and they take what these celebrities say as though it is Me. They take a leader of a great nation, and they expose what they think they have been able to make look like the truth, and most of you swallow it. If they choose, they hide what others do and expose only what they want to persuade you in their corner of thinking, and if you were praying for your leaders as I instructed you in My Word, you never would have helped them destroy the president, and you would have seen it and prayed for it. Many leaders of the past did much worse, and none of it was ever exposed. Leaders are human beings, and all humans are flawed. Knowing this, My great love constantly strives to lead them to repentance. This man has a great deal of love for his country and its people no matter what you think. Some of you are so foolish that you permit the media to control your thinking, and had you gone into My Word, you would have recognized through God-given discernment what to do. Some of you who have gone to church for years and years stand before the world and say, "I don't know who to vote for, I have to pray." To the one who knows My Word, it is very clear not to ever put a person in office that destroys another human being and calls it right. Yes, you have choices; on one hand you see your life as you know it financially slipping away from you, and you will choose someone you think who will be your savior where your money is concerned. Live deliciously, live with ease, able to go anywhere, or do anything at any time like I have always blessed you is one of your choices; the other is to destroy the innocent. Tell me, how is that choice picking up your cross and denying yourself anything? In the end, which choice do you think I will be pleased with?

I will not defend him because he is right; I will not defend him because he is perfect or because he hasn't made any mistakes. He claims My name and has made as many mistakes *as those of you who are calling to destroy him have made*. Why do any of you think that I did not destroy completely some of your former leaders? Was it because any of them were perfect? Was it because any man is worthy of being worshipped? It is because just as you would be in a marriage and in order for you to have your way, you have to destroy the spouse? In that small realm of marriage, you then sever your right arm off. And you bleed for a long, long time. Both are guilty in the marriage because being one, you are not fully to blame on either side. So it is in this nation with its leaders, never is the full blame on them.

Your support in prayer, your blessings in speech and not curses would have turned all of this around. You all will answer to Me for not holding up your leaders in prayer. Yes, I love justice. *But I hate it when those who are unjust call for it*. I hate it when those who are not without sin expect Me to deliver someone into their hands. Those who deliberately go against My Word and make a mockery of what it says in My children, I do not support such people. But when one is faithful enough to stand up and say they believe in the sanctity of a marriage between a man and a woman, when they believe and confess it to the world that they are against killing innocent babies, then *I will stand up and protect them.* But when a man and a woman fight to give anyone the right to kill an innocent human being or fight to give marriage rights to those of the same sex, I most definitely will not defend them, nor will I stand up for them, for they have forsaken My word. *And I will never go against My Word* because *My Word is Jesus Christ.* Therefore, when you choose them over Me, well, ask yourself, will I be with you when you need Me? Only for a season will Satan seem to give you comfort and take care of you because he knows your end. So if you seem to succeed, remember My Word is true, and I have no darkness at all in Me.

I stand up for this man in exactly the same way that you want Me to stand up for you. If I dealt with you as harshly as you would have dealt with those who needed you to help them, to support them, and you deserted them, there would be nothing left of you. If life, the elements, and every force that Satan can send against you became the judgment that you so desire on him, then I tell you right now, there would be nothing left of you. Judgment is easy to dish out. Why do you think I speak out against gainsayers, scorners, faultfinders, and such like? Because I hate all those evil works. I hate the works of the flesh that claim to have Me on their side. You never walked in the shoes of the man that you lie on and condemn. You have no idea what it is like. You strive and fight to obtain, and when you do, there is every evil work just as it says in My Word in the book of James. I show mercy to those who show mercy. You say he has no mercy? I say when did I die and make you God enough to judge what is in a man's heart? You have a right to see the fruits, but you have no right to destroy. You let criminals go free, but you destroy many good men that I have sent to lead in the past. You don't care that a criminal mind has murdered; you just care that they not have to pay, so it is all right if they deny, deny, deny, and never admit they did anything. You pray and pray and pray that a murderer go free because you have pity on him; he belongs to your group. Your counselors tell them as Christians to never admit their wrongs to anyone. And you believe that I Am with you to cover all the evil up and give restitution, or at least godly sorrow is never expressed. You think and feel justified as though I justified you. You forget, justification can only come with a humble and contrite heart, admitting your sin, *never denying it*. And you're still doing that today. You need to hope I do not treat him the way you think that I should because if I would need to, I would visit you *first*. And to all of you, he who is without sin, cast the first stone.

Do you rejoice when you think you caught someone at something? Do you rejoice when you are able to destroy someone and make them look as dirty as your mind? Do you get excited at the fact that you are able to make your money by destroying someone? And do you claim that I am with you? Because if you do, remember I take up no cause to destroy anyone in this nation on your ability to destroy. You are on your own.

I will not prophesy to you who is going to win any election because I refuse to foretell the future. What happens to this nation depends on your choice. You will have no one to blame once you put whom you desire in office. A prophet's job is much, much more than telling the future, even though a prophet can and does do that. Some of you have the mind of those who run from place to place, looking for someone to tell a future for you. What difference is there between you and a person who seeks a fortune-teller? I sent prophecy to *warn* you of what is up ahead for you if you do not repent. This is why they were hated in the past because they told the truth, and they warned people to repent. They were not used to comfort those who were sinning. A prophet that comforts more than he can be used to warn is no profit to Me and the cause of Christ. When you give comforting prophecies for all, remember that not all who claim to be Mine are Mine. One of the most important things for prophecy is to *warn*. If I could not speak to you through prophecy, then how can you see you're wrong and repent? Especially in this hour where so many have turned off the Word. Jesus told what was to come for this world. That was not His whole ministry. He rebuked and exhorted all through the New Testament. First when He walked on the earth and then through those that are His. You need to hear His voice in this hour upon the earth right now; His voice through those who are His can still be heard if you listen.

If you have an interest in only yourself so much that you go to every altar just to hear a Word from Me about you, then I do not want any part of you unless you repent. If you go to a church simply to be used where others can see, then I have no need or use for you. If you give or do anything simply because you want to have peace that you are doing what I told you, you are still border lining being useless. If you come with a pure heart, one that desires to deny itself and do My will at any cost, then I might be able to begin to use you.

Your judgment of Me means nothing to Me. I do exactly what I chose to do with what is Mine, and I right now tell you that it is not My will for any of you to dare touch judgment where the leader of your nation is concerned. You think he did wrong? Tell it to Me and you know what I will tell you, exactly what *you* are doing wrong. Why? Because where he is, what he is doing, what he does is none of your business. It is My business. I have the power to cause what belongs to me to stand or fall. Your job is to pull down Satan and his works. Never was it ever to pull down people. Your job is to bind Satan when you see his works. Never is it or was it ever to touch the hair on the head of anyone who believes in Me. It is better for a millstone to be tied around the neck of the person who hurts one of these little ones who believe in Me. I call them *all* My children. And since you don't sit in My seat and you don't see what I see and you are disobedient, who are you?

Those of you who are self-righteous, those who pay too much attention to what you hear without ever being there have no clue as to what is really going on, you go by what you hear, and I told you to judge righteous judgment, not according to what you hear or even see. I never condemned you for the loss of My Son for you. Never did I get angry with you because you had sinned so much. He was without *any* sin, and I gave Him up freely that you may be free, and now you are demanding that someone else not be free. Where do you think this will take you? I never rose up and fought in a rage of anger and hatred against any of you. Never did I speak out and tell everyone all the things that you did in secret when you asked Me to forgive you. I *covered it with My Son's blood*. I promise you now that every one of you who is determined to bring harm or see to it that someone pays for what you think they did or are doing, I promise you that what you do and have done will be exposed. What people hear in the ear will be shouted upon the housetops about you. Just about the hour that you think you have everything all sowed up, remember *I Am God*.

Your pride, self-righteousness, foolishness, and silliness are delivering up this nation to your enemies. As God, I have the right to be outraged and angry for you being forgiven while My Son paid, and I never was, nor will I be. And now you are being guilty, desiring another to pay. Are you so much without wisdom that you cannot see? The young men and women who gave their lives and their bodies willingly suffer more with your erasing the reason that they gave their lives. Don't you understand you *erase* their sacrifice and force them to feel as though what they did was in vain, when I called them to the purpose of protecting *you*? You erase My Son's life through disobedience by not putting His Word into your heart and mind or by applying the negative of the Word to everyone but yourself. If there is one soldier, man, or woman who gave their life or their body to answer the call of this nation and you do these things that dishonor them, then it is on you. Even if you lost a child in any war for this country, you are dishonoring their loss, and it is on you.

Who are these people who enjoy the freedom of this country, the protection of it, and speak evil of it? Why would you watch them at all? Why do you give them a voice by watching what they think, what they feel? All their excuses and reasons to justify themselves because they are afraid that they must face Me in the end; therefore, they must destroy the truth in you. And you are so foolish that you enjoy them.

Who are these who once knew Me and rejected Me? Even the enemy that you cannot seem to find, he once knew Me and turned on Me. Who is he that he could remain not captured while you blame someone else for your lack of faith and prayer to bring him to justice? But then Judas knew My Son also, and he turned on Him also. You sit seemingly safe now, but when it invades you, then you will understand. You depend on your youth now; you depend on your looks, your ways, your success, your accomplishments, and your abilities, never realizing that in one day all can disappear. Those of you who claim anyone is unjust have become unjust in order to proclaim it. You become exactly what you claim the other is. You see it within another because it is deep within you. And the only way to see that is to look directly into the mirror of the Word and repent. If you are unjust, you will fight and hate to obtain what really doesn't belong to you. If it belonged to you, it would have been yours long, long time ago. I would have given it to you gladly. But no, to obtain it without all this hatred and evil thinking is too difficult; so you try to obtain it by claiming you, poor you, were robbed. I tell you now, you robbed yourself. When you fight against what I have not chosen to remove, who are you fighting against? And if I Am the only One who could remove it, then why do you fight? No soul is converted or changed until I convert them. And if they are not doing what you think is so necessary, why do you get offended if they don't have what you do? Do you honestly believe that Jesus hated people who were not like Him? Do you honestly believe that He would approve of what you are doing? If you truly do not make a difference between you and another, then why do you speak of the difference? All deny that they are doing that. Both sides, the media, all deny that they do this. And all the while they speak about white, black, red, yellow, or blue, they are all guilty of doing it. And all of you are like little kids in kindergarten pointing out each other's faults as though no one can really see you. As men and as women, you play games with the country, the world, and the lives you are to be responsible for. All of you do these things, not one, but all. When it comes to your national security, I want you to know that this nation is no game. This hour is no game.

I do not have to tell you the sins of this nation. What I do have to tell you is to come out of it. Come out of the things that you have allowed to touch your life. The only way out is to come out of those sins. I Am still stronger than your enemies. Do not permit them to paralyze you with fear. Do not let them intimidate you to fight. With patience, with wisdom, and with understanding—those are your stability, believing that no matter who wants to continue to destroy this nation, *I Am not with them.* And if I Am not with someone, then the result will be seen. My Word says that you are to keep yourself from the paths of the destroyer. You will never tell Me anything about what is a destroyer and what isn't because I made him. I know that his desire is to kill a person who loves Me; and My Word could never kill anyone unless it was in defense of his home, his family, or his country. After all, it is only Satan that threatens your nation. It isn't Me. I am not with them. When I see the blood of My Son Jesus Christ, I will pass over you. But if I don't see it, how then can I pass? These words are not speaking about war, for there are times that we must go to war, and war is always ugly. To defend this great nation, some things have to be done in spite of all of her enemies within.

The celebrities that take the young are not of Me. It is no marvel that a young person is tempted to be deceived. People who go after the young people know they are taking advantage of the young who do not understand. They know they are deliberately deceiving them, and they seek to use them. Don't be deceived.

If you raised a great young person with the truth, then stand firm in the belief that Satan cannot take them. If you see them striving toward Me and they lack the understanding that you have, then stand firm in the blood of Jesus to keep them from his clutch, instead of feeding it by believing that Satan can take what belongs to Me. You raise a young person and teach them all about Me. Then they go to college, and some professor who imagines they are something teaches them the opposite of all they have ever learned, and it sometimes sticks. But it doesn't need to. You could not imagine the evil that is in some of these colleges.

If you are one of the young, know this: I will never tear down My order of things. Every person must first be led in order to lead. Every person is led by somebody. Your mind answers the call of whatever you willingly expose yourself to. If you expose yourself to the wrong and then one day you decide to change, you forget there are consequences. Those consequences cannot be prayed away. They have to be changed by making them right. By admitting the wrong and making it right with others. They cannot be covered up; they must be dealt with and changed. I erase the sin and forget it *after* you make it right. The world tells you that it all must be fair and balanced. I tell you plainly to obey My Word and put your moral convictions above those who you think you are going to save. I tell you to know that the moment of conception is life. Life is in the blood. I will hold everyone responsible who takes life lightly, so lightly that they can support someone who gives the right to choose to kill.

If you have ever been at the deathbed of someone and the doctors tell you that they are on life support, that blood is being pumped through their veins and they are going to cut the system off because the brain is dead. Life is not in the brain. It is in the blood. I have raised brain-dead people up to prove it. The life everyone chooses to destroy so easily *will bring something upon your life that you are not prepared to handle.*

I sent you parents from the time you were little to teach you how to obey the things that I set up. If you read in Romans chapter 1 (KJV) how that I wrote in one sentence to obey your parents right alongside with a comma in between, next to words like "murder." In order for you to break away, you must murder the spirit of your parents; and I do not take that lightly, especially if you were raised in a Christian home, especially if your parents are godly. It is only My grace that keeps them alive. This isn't a matter of age; this isn't a matter of a difference of opinion. *This is a matter of your life.* The blessings you enjoy as a Christian coming from a Christian home came at a great price from your parents. And you honestly believe that I would lead you against that? Because you think you see something in a person, or you heard someone who claims to be Mine, or the media says something good about them? If you claim to be Mine, then I set up leaders who know My Word, who have lived longer than you, and who understand far beyond your years. You are capable of making a greater mistake than what you see the elders are making. You may be determined to change this country, and because you are young, you think that you can. I warn you that the change can never be against My Word.

And those of you who have come from a dysfunctional home and have given your life to Me, I want you to remember you cannot deny Me and still have Me. I will never put My stamp of approval on murder. You say it is murder to let someone be poor or go to war. I say that you do not know, nor do you see what you are talking about. Adults make choices, they choose to marry the same gender, and they choose to destroy a child in their belly. And a helpless child has no such choice;

they are destroyed before they are born, and you call that a good cause and think because a person sounds good that I would be with this?

I urge you to come to Me, and do not make such a decision without the presence of My Spirit. And I *promise you that you will never* feel My Presence on the choice to toss away what I taught you in My Word; killing the innocent is murder. You *must* take a stand against it, and that stand is by *never* supporting anyone who believes this is right. I do not say speak out against it, I do not say lift a finger against it. But I do say taste not, touch not, handle not. Come out from among their thinking. Come out from among the agreement with them that they can be the savior of your world. I Am with no one who takes a stand with violence, *no one, for no reason could ever turn Me to deliberately destroy someone else.* Those who have chosen to fight through bombing clinics are not of Me. You become what you hate. The self-righteousness that lies to you tells you that certain things are all right to do, that I will still be with you. I tell you all right now, *never*! You chose murder when you chose to support someone who thinks nothing of murdering a defenseless person. And if that fact doesn't stir you, then you need to examine your heart in My presence.

People who are in the public eye through music, through movies, or any such like do not have a conscience where *your* life is concerned. If they did, they would never make some of the evil things that they do. They do not even let their own children watch what they make because they know how evil it is. Like pied pipers, they play a tune to the young. And with smooth talk and a smile, they say nice things; or they know how to speak, how to pretend. And you lift them as high as heaven and worship the ground they walk on. And when true trouble comes, *let us see if they can save you, and let us see if they will. When the attraction of their beauty fades, where do you suppose they go? Who can help them?*

And some of you who are older support them because they are either your gender or your ethnic group. And *none* of you can see how evil this is for you. There are women that I consider Mine that would never touch some of the things that are being done today. There are men who are Mine that would not touch destroying any helpless individual. But you cannot see who they are, and you know why? You never pay

46

attention to what is going on around you, and when that sweep from the enemy comes, you will listen to the individual who can persuade you. Not to the one who would never do things against Me.

I blame those who call themselves by My name and refuse to get into the Word and seek Me. I blame them that the politicians get away with all the lying and cheating and stealing in order to get elected, and it seems if they don't do that, they can't win. I hold a lot of the people accountable to Me for not doing their homework, and at the midnight hour expect me to reveal to them whom they should choose. If you knew My Word, you would see the fruits that destroy innocent babies are not of Me.

It isn't just a matter of praying before you vote. You are like a man who goes to work every day, and because he has worked all day, he sits like a king after work and tells himself that nothing else should be required of him. He has no real responsibilities, no part in raising the children and being a person who cares not about what goes on in his wife's life or his children's. All he wants to do is come home and play like a little kid. It is with this kind of attitude that people vote. They did their part; all that should be required of them. And many of them pray for their heroes in sports and never pray for their country's condition. And they blame everyone else. Can you see why it is in trouble today? Your responsibility goes far beyond what you think you see that you seem to be accomplishing.

PART III

"In the beginning was the Word, and the Word was with God, and the Word was God. The same was in the beginning with God. All things were made by Him; and without Him was not anything made that was made. In Him was life; and the life was the light of men. And the light shineth in darkness; and the darkness comprehended it not" (John 1:1-5).

Being in the flesh it is difficult for you to understand how precious Jesus is to My heart. All of you think you know it but you don't. I will honor Him above all. You must do so also by honoring His Words. 1 Peter 4:17 "For the time is come that judgment must begin at the house of God and if it begin at us, what shall the end be of them that obey not the gospel of God? And if the righteous scarcely be saved, where shall the ungodly and sinner appear? And when the time comes to deal with all these things, I will look down from heaven, and I will see His blood applied to the soul of those who took His Word to their heart and allowed the Holy Spirit to lead, guide, and direct them into all truth in the Word. After all, I Am the Spirit of Truth. I do desire those to worship Me in the Spirit and in the Truth. And I warn all of you who claim My name (you know the name Christian?), who claim My Word (you know My Word called the Bible, called the Word in John 1:1?),

48

who claim My Holy Spirit (you know "the Spirit of Truth"?). Get into the Word and read as much as you can of it. Make an achievable goal and read at first a chapter or two a day, and as you get comfortable with that amount and it becomes a good habit, add a couple more chapters, and when you grow from there, add more. For I make a promise to you right now that when I come, if I do not see the blood of Jesus Christ applied to your heart, I will not pass over you. *For the blood can only be applied through having the Word of God written on the tables of your heart. And the only way that can be done is to read it. This is the message that is going to be preached across the world before I come.* This message is very plain, very simple to understand, and the most valuable lesson that you will ever allow yourself to learn. Meditate upon My Word, ponder all the things that I Am saying within those precious pages. Now is the hour in your life that you must use your faith to get the Word within you. Let Jesus live and breathe within you. The New Testament is the beginning of teaching you My will. It has to be a living, breathing part of you through living it. Everything else that you will ever understand is not as important as this is to you right now. Look at the Word and see it to be *the most important, the most valuable part of your life; look at it as though you can never enter into heaven without knowing it, living it, understanding it, loving it, feeding off of the "Bread of Life."* Some of you have never lived it; you live only parts of it, the parts that you chose.

As you reject My Words, I will reject you. As you fill your life up with what you so choose within your heart and your soul, so will I fill up your life with what you choose. I will *never* separate My Word which *is Jesus Christ* from the Holy Spirit that I put in the heart of every person who has been converted by accepting Jesus as their personal Savior. You made a commitment with Me when you asked Me to come into your heart. You made a covenant that for some of you, *only I kept. I kept My promise,* and *I gave you the Holy Spirit. I kept My covenant and promise,* and *I gave you My Word. I kept My promise,* and *I gave you access to My Throne in the name of Jesus Christ.* And many of you *never* kept *your* part of the agreement. *You still refuse to go into My Word and learn of Me.* And My people perish because of their lack of knowledge. You have a vision *for this life.* That vision is selfish and fulfills your desires if you have not picked up your cross daily and obeyed the Word. I promised that what is not of Me will fall. Look around you. See if I Am with you or not. If you see I Am not, then repent and trim your lamp with the anointing that can only come in the *Word through the power of the Holy Spirit.*

You don't understand buying and selling? Did I not say there would be those who would make merchandise of you? Did I not warn you that there would be those who have their own bellies in mind when they persuade you away from My Word and *not into* My Word? The day truly will come when you will be so foolish as to ask Me, "Did I not prophesy in Your name? Did I not do many wonderful works in Your name?" And I will definitely tell you depart from Me, ye that work iniquity. Because in that day, you are so blind that you cannot see that you are coming to Me, trusting in the things that *you* built upon. The things that *you* think *you* have done to earn your way into heaven, to earn even prosperity here on earth. To prophesy is what Jesus did; it was not evil. To do many wonderful works and to cast out devils are exactly what Jesus did. Why would He call it working iniquity? *Because you depend upon your gifts to get you into heaven instead of depending upon the blood of Jesus Christ.* My Holy Spirit's main purpose is to lead you into all truth *in the Word, in Jesus.* My gift of My Spirit was never intended to prove that you are of Me without ever truly being of Me. You could not imagine how many are depending upon their gift, as though it is the gift that buys your way into heaven when the only way into heaven is the acceptance of Jesus Christ. You say that you cannot be gifted without being in Jesus. They do exactly as they chose with their private lives, even sin in secret and believe because I use them, it is all going to be all right. You call that grace. My *grace* was never intended to continue in sin. Matthew 1:21 (KJV) says, "And she shall bring forth a son, and thou shalt call His name JESUS: for He shall save His people *from their sins.*" It was never intended to take Me in the places that you want to go. My grace was intended to cause Jesus to live so much within you that you could not willfully and deliberately sin against Me. Since My gifts and calling are without repentance, you can use them and still fall from grace. Because you depend upon that gift which you are able to use. *That gift was never given for you. It was given for all others.* This is why dying daily is so important; you blaspheme so easily. Make Me look like a fool; make me look like a liar and a cheat.

You don't see it, do you? You don't see those who refuse to live the way they ought are still able to do all things that they had from the beginning of their walk because My gifts are without repentance. So if a preacher steps down off of the pulpit and he beats his wife afterward, he still goes behind the pulpit, able to preach or teach. This is no secret, this is no mystery. Many of you know of those who have fallen. What many of you don't know is that because they are able to go on doesn't mean that I am blessing them. It only means that I keep My word, I keep My promise, and I will use them at times. But all will have to face Me in the end. True repentance brings true forgiveness. Jesus died to save you *from your sins, never to keep you in them.* And if you believe that you cannot stop sinning as long as you walk on this earth, then you do not believe My Word. *Because if you die daily to live My Word, Jesus would be so powerful in you that you could never do the things that you do now.* But it costs so much to die daily for you that you receive the deception and think that you will enter into heaven. It is easier to say that we all sin in some way every day. A heart that loves Me, My Word, and My Spirit can never do that. There is not a sin, no matter how evil, no matter how seemingly small, that cannot be overcome. You were to overcome it all in you first, then teach others how to live like Jesus. I Am not speaking of every person who claims My name. If you are not doing these things, if you do not willfully and deliberately accept that you have to sin, then happy are ye. Keep those things that I have taught you. To all others, I say repent. Cry out to Me to be free, and I will set you free. That cry from the beginning of your salvation journey was to continue until it was finished, for I Am the author and the finisher of your faith. And the *beginning continues until the end.*

I told you plainly to eat My flesh and drink My blood. The Word *is all* the blood of Jesus Christ, and the Word *is also all* of the "Bread of Life," which is Jesus Christ, and yet many of you have put it on a shelf and left the ability to understand it in another's hands. You needed to read it yourself. You needed to pray for yourself. You needed your personal relationship with Me. Not depending on anyone else to get it

51

for you or give it to you. This was, and is, and has been between you and Me. This gift of the Holy Spirit which was given to you at conversion, and this gift was *given to lead you into the Word and cause the Word to abide within you*. Through you, each and every one of you I intended to do many mighty miracles to see many souls saved. So many of you are satisfied with what little you have, and as Paul said, you turned to weak and beggarly things. You run to others to intercede for you when there is only *one mediator* between God and man, and His name is Jesus Christ. As long as the flesh is abiding in you, then you corrupt everything that I intended for you. The Holy Spirit was to operate through you, without ever being hindered, and the only purpose for that was to give glory to Jesus Christ. That is the *only* way that I can abide within you. And if you put the Word off daily, you put My Son off daily. And the time will come when you will want to play "catch-up," and it will be too late, so I Am telling you now that all the self-help books, all the preaching and teaching cannot put that personal relationship with Jesus Christ within you. The only way you can have it is by living on the "Bread of Life," not by reading little pieces of Him daily to accomplish your desires. Living means just that, living within you. Oh, you say that He is your personal savior, and you tell everyone about it. You lift up your hands toward heaven and ask Him to come into your heart; and when the time comes to know Him in His Word, you put Him in His place in your life, on a shelf. Most of you do this, except when you want something, and then you put that part in you. The time is at hand to repent of these things, especially those of you who claim to be My prophets.

So I ask you plainly, I plead with you in My love, in the love that I had for you so much that My Son died to take you into heaven with Him; I ask you to repent of giving glory to anyone but the One who died for you. For I promised you that *every knee shall bow, every tongue confess that Jesus Christ is LORD*. Do you understand that a Lord rules, reigns, and controls you? And if Jesus hasn't done that through His Word in you, it is because you would not put Him in there to do so; and then ask yourself a question, where are you? And who are you following? Think about all the years that I gave you upon this earth with opportunity to put the Word into your heart and your mind. Think about how many times I sent someone to preach and teach and you felt you did not have to because you were wrapped safely and securely in your religion or in a ministry. And your religion doesn't have the power to take you into heaven, neither does your ministry. And some of you have the audacity to tell Me that you know what My Word says. You read it, and you now know everything. There is only one way. Jesus said, "I Am the Truth, the Life, and the Way. No man can come to the Father but by Me." But you listened to someone who claimed they read the Word, and you accepted what they said even when it went against the words that were deliberately written in red to stand out so that you would have no excuse. They were quotes of Jesus Christ, and those words say, "In vain do they worship Me teaching doctrines of men."

When you are taught that once you give your life to Jesus you are always in Jesus no matter what you do, that you cannot lose your salvation, you need to go into the Word and read in Hebrews that you can lose your day of grace by tramping on the blood of Jesus Christ and that it is a fearful thing to fall into the hands of the Living God for doing so. Or did you take what someone else told you about what it all said? How foolish is that? You didn't search it out for yourself. What a chance you take with eternity. You come close to tramping on His blood when you count the Word as nothing. When you do this in ignorance, and I come and tell you, then you need to let Me to begin to work with you to help you face up to your responsibility to the Word. Never did I intend for you to take comfort in being able to count My Son's blood as something so worthless and powerless that you cannot cease from sin or want to.

Look at your hands, and where do they go? Look at your feet, where do they go? When I said if your hand offends you, cut it off. You are so foolish that I must not have meant that. The cutting off isn't a physical thing. Whatever you are into that causes your hand to sin, you are to cut that out of your life. How swiftly do they run to shed innocent blood? Do you run to tell everyone what your neighbor seems to be doing? Do you run to spread things to make yourself look good and another look evil?

Look at your heart and see where it has been. How swiftly does it judge and condemn your brother? I said to be swift to hear and slow to speak, but I never said be swift to hear or see what another is doing so that you can be swift to judge someone. Therein is My hatred, for brother rises up against brother and devours each other and calls it a blessing from Me. And you are so foolish that you think this is what I intended when I made this nation great to glorify Me.

This nation was not made great because of the people who formed it. Although many were Mine, and their obedience to Me was and is their greatness, it was made great *because it is the only nation who always stood with Israel.* There were those who read the Word and believed the Word and obeyed the Word. I promised that I would bless those who blessed Israel and that I would curse those who cursed Israel. And because in your flesh you have not seemed to see the blessing or the curse, it is no matter to Me. I do exactly as I chose with what belongs to Me. I chose them, just as I chose the true believing Christian. I called them, just as I called those who love My Son. And if you become offended with these facts, then I suggest you read the Word, for they say word for word what is being written here in this book. I ordained it, I decided it, I will bring all things to performance according to My Word, and no one will change it no matter what it looks like now or has looked like. I said that I chose you; you did not choose Me. Peter confessed that Jesus is the Son of the Living God. Jesus told him plainly that flesh and blood did not reveal that to him. It came directly from My Throne; *so if you believe that Jesus Christ is My Son, and that I raised Him from the dead, then I personally revealed that to you. I personally chose you to belong to My Son.*

The floodgates have opened, and hell has enlarged herself. And My angels are ready with their sickles. *Come out, My children. Come out from anything or anyone who leads you to believe one thing against My Word.* Remain with those who faithfully and honestly and truthfully have told you what is in the Word and warned you to get into it and obey My Son. For today is the day of salvation. Today is the day unlike any other. For the time is short and no games will be played; I Am right now drawing a line. I Am right now writing in My book those who obey and those who refuse. You will not see it in the flesh. You will not hear it in the flesh. But those who are Mine will see and hear. I Am not speaking of what your leaders have told you that My Word says. I Am speaking about you getting into a church where they preach salvation, *not* religion. Not church history and lie that it is the only true church, and if you don't belong to it and obey its doctrine, then you are not going to make it to heaven. I promise you today that if you do not belong to My Son Jesus Christ through having His blood applied to your sins, you have no part in Me. Read My Word, no one has the power to forgive you of sin except Jesus Christ, because no one else died for you. No one can cause you to pay penance for your sins. No amount of praying, no amount of anything can ever erase your sin except asking God for the blood of Jesus Christ to erase it by forgiving you.

And I warn you, do not twist this up to mean that if you wear pants and you are a woman you are not of Me, if you wear makeup and you are a woman you are not of Me. I taught in My word to dress modestly, that means cover your body. You taught and believed in extremes in clothing, hair, etc. You taught that the skirts have to be down to the floor and the neckline has to be up the neck. I did not teach that; no man has a right to condemn you or tell you that you are not welcome in church. If you are so ignorant that you dress almost naked and expose your breasts or your thighs, then the sin is yours, repent; these things are paid so much attention to that it takes away from the truth of the gospel. If you are preaching against religions, against people, against anyone, then you are not preaching the gospel. My church needs to be taught how to allow Jesus to live within their hearts and minds.

While you were busy deciding things like wearing pants and women not having roles in the church, there are many souls that were being destroyed in this country. While you busied yourselves with things that have no real meaning such as women not being able to preach, children were being destroyed because the most important things were being neglected while you fought over nothing. Children were raped looking for a savior, their own parents turning on them, and you were too busy for Me to call into intercessory prayer. You were fighting over nothing.

55

PART IV

"And as they did eat, He said, Verily I say unto you, that one of you shall betray Me. And they were exceeding sorrowful, *and began every one of them to say unto Him, Lord, is it I?* And He answered and said, he that dippeth his hand with Me in the dish, the same shall betray Me" (Matthew 26:21-23 KJV).

These men were His apostles, and they walked and talked and lived and breathed their life with Him. They heard things that we have yet to hear. They were given understanding and truths that we still have yet to learn. And yet every one of them said to Him, "Lord, is it I?" They had the Word every day. They walked with Him and listened to Him for hours, days, and years. And yet at that moment, none knew their own heart. Each one at times had to be told and explained in detail the parables. He questioned them, are they yet without understanding? Still, after all this time that He spent with them, are they still without understanding? He did not get angry with them. He did not hate them, He did not punish them, but He most certainly did deal with them. He knew that the consequences of their own actions would be punishment enough. When you saw that Peter wept because he denied Jesus three times, were you able to see how Peter must have felt? Peter would have rather died than to be found doing this, but it happened because Peter did not know what was in his own heart at that time. Jesus knew. Even when the truth hurt, He spoke it plainly and clearly lest any of you should misunderstand. Are you going to now be wise enough to ask, "Lord, is it I?" Every one of you that has not the Word abiding in you is capable of betraying Me. In an hour that you are sure that you will not deny Me, you can and perhaps will. *Peter was positive* that he would never betray Jesus, but he did, and so will you if you do not fill up with the Word.

Today protect your soul, protect your vessel, and protect yourself through the Word. When you have Jesus Christ within in the Word, the Word rises up on the occasion of temptation that you need to overcome everything. How can He resurrect in you and keep you the way He promised if you will not ever let Him in?

I have heard many preach and teach and talk about those who walked with My Son or talked with Him in the garden, and each time it was with so little respect. Not realizing that any one of you is capable of betraying Me without My Word within you. *Hear what I Am going to say and do not say it to anyone as though I said this is speaking of any particular person.* Because right now, at this moment, I Am the only person who knows who is spoken of in the book of Revelation.

Everyone wonders if the Antichrist is living on the earth today. They look for signs, and they do not realize that they are looking in all the wrong places. According to the scriptures, he has to emerge after walking and talking with Jesus the way Judas did. He will know Him and then turn on Him. In order to betray Me, he will know a lot about Jesus. I Am not telling you that he will know a lot about religion. I am saying that he will know a lot about Jesus. He will have walked and talked with My disciples. He will be convinced in the end that he knows better than what he was taught of Me. He will turn slowly the way Judas did and ripen for the hour. He will betray Jesus for money the way Judas did. He will have been in on everything that God was doing and then go to those who thought they were in control and betray by telling all he heard and knew. He will be a pretender in his heart and find no real value in the Word even though he claims to have it. He will have the right words at the right time and know how to act, how to overcome, how to do things to *appear* as though he has Jesus Christ within him. He will even on occasion confess Jesus. He will have no passion in his heart for it. He will be sure that he knows it because he has read it and sat under preaching that looks and sounds so much like the truth. He will have belonged to a ministry that is as self-seeking as he is. It will be so close that only Mine will see it. Mine will know the hour that it turns; they will see it just before it happens. Just as Jesus knew which one was going to betray Him, those that have Jesus within them will know who he is. He will not be a man of religion. He will claim to know salvation. He will slowly see himself as a Savior. At first he will think that he is of Me. Then the power within his hands will corrupt him the way Satan was corrupted by his own beauty and power. Any man on earth could be put in power, and this never happens. But this one will be appointed. Listen to what I tell you. There are many Antichrists, and they all begin with some knowledge of Me through the knowledge of the Word. And they break out of the Word and make everything the way they want. They will be self-seeking and very able to accomplish it. And this is done even today in so many ways. Many of those ways are spoken about constantly in this book. Self-, self-, self-centeredness finally took Judas. This man will take everything as though it belongs to him. He will not know who he is, that is why it will not be revealed until the time. Judas didn't know until the time. I Am the only One who knows the time.

He will have no regard for women. That doesn't necessarily mean that he will like men; that doesn't mean that he is openly against women. He could be married. Because it could perhaps only mean that he doesn't know that in Christ there is no man, and no woman, that I did not set a difference. It could mean that he accepts no woman as having the power or the right to preach or be able to pastor or to be a leader of any organization or nation. He will not consider what they think or feel. It could mean that he thinks a woman's place is in the home taking care of her children and that I would never use her as a prophet, as a leader of any country. Consider what I am telling you! Those of you who know the Word will know what I am saying. Your headship as a man gives you power over your wife to rebuke the enemy and protect her from any onslaught against your family and your calling which includes her. I made no man lord over his wife. I gave him no power to dictate to her how she should serve Me when I call her. I gave no man special permission to mistreat her or abuse her verbally or to abuse her by treating her as though she is so much less than him. I did clearly say that her body is yours and your body is hers. Never did I say that you were to take My Son's place over her with her calling. Ask yourself, do you honestly believe that a man is greater than a woman? Or do you know that I make no difference just as I make no difference with color, where you live, or even your church if it is preaching the gospel? If you line up with Me, then I line up with you. When I say I make no difference, I mean no difference; I do not call them because they are one color in particular or came from a suffering, hardship, culture, or gender. I Am no respecter of persons. Everyone who obeys My Word is the same to Me. And if you claim Me, remember a past is not something that you simply brush under the rug and pretend nothing ever happened and believe that I will cover it for you. It is something that you work out by repenting, and that takes admitting you did what you did. You can never say it is personal, just between you and Me, if you ever hurt anyone including an innocent child.

This vessel sat in the pew of a church and saw two huge angels striving against each other. Each one was taking a stand. One strove and shoved the other. They strove very hard to push each other off of their stand. Each shove was felt within her. One would seem to gain ground, but the feet were firmly planted, so like two wrestlers they could only shove. She sat there unable to cry, unable to pray, and even after the experience, unable to speak to any person about it for many years. Because up until today (which is July 20, 2008), she did not understand what she saw. Her mouth was bound, unable to speak; her hands were bound behind her back, unable to use them in prayer. She strove so hard to be free. It almost took her physical life, and it almost took her soul, for she could feel both the physical life almost die and the spiritual life at the brink. And there was nothing that she could do; she did not know what to do. Even though she suffered tremendously just watching it, she could see herself bound and gagged. And now she realizes that it was the Jesus within her that was bound and gagged by the church. That struggle was a fight for the pulpit. Not the pulpit of that particular church but *the* church. Brother against brother, each one claiming that I Am with them.

Are you so foolish even now to think that all of this is written against My church? No, this is written *for My church*. The light has been turned on, not for others to see, but *for you in your personal relationship with Me*. Never would I reveal even one truth in this book if I did not intend to protect you, keep you, strengthen you, help you to not only overcome but be more victorious in your life than you ever have been before. Never do I ever reveal anything that seems negative in a warning without showing you the way out. Never would I ever speak so harshly seemingly at times if it wasn't for the fact that some of you need it so much. Anything I say to you is for you to use as an opportunity to get it all right. Never to make you get so low with it that you cannot get up. It is never to condemn you but only to convict you. Because I have a place for you all planned out. A place that you will want to be with Me. *I have a plan for you, and it is not for evil but for good for you.* My arms are open wide, waiting for you to come to Me. If you know all these things, then as the scripture says, "Happy are ye."

This church that she saw this war in had a spirit that was released within it. She doesn't remember the exact occasion, but she will *never* forget what she felt. She was told it was a Judas spirit. It had a tremendous impact; she could feel it so strongly. Put it in the light of the warring angels and this release, and you can understand it. There was no such thing as rebuking this spirit. *It manifested* for one purpose to be recognized, only to be seen as to what it was. Some things you can pray all day long, and if they are ordained by Me, then I Am not looking for you to rebuke it. What I Am looking for is for you to *obey the Word through it. Dying to self is your only path to freedom, through obedience to Jesus Christ. You must die to yourself and let Jesus live. It can never work if you only think you know who Jesus is; remember I said this for this is important to your soul. You must know Him.*

And most of all, this woman never even to this day prays any other way but "Thy will be done." And she never presumes what that will is. Only in My Presence will she receive any word. And only in My Presence will she pray, knowing it is safe to pray. Those of you who have the Spirit of God within you will ask, 'Is it I, Lord," because it will be clear that you may not know your own heart; and this is why in this hour, it is very important to know it enough to pray. To ask if there be anything within you that doesn't belong and be willing to accept the fact that if there is and you recognize it, then it isn't you. You can seek forgiveness and repent.

Notice that none of them ever asked Jesus *which one*; they asked Him, "Is it I?" Therefore, they knew and understood that He would *never* talk about anybody to them. He did not say one word until the time. And that was only because he wanted them to see it when it came to pass and to pray for Him. Hear what I am saying. Stop and pray over this. It is a true revelation. The abomination that makes you desolate is something that makes the soul desolate. And nothing makes the soul more desolate than rejecting the Word which is Jesus, claiming Jesus and having some other way to get into heaven. Or taking a part of what He did say in the Word and taking it as your own. Watch and pray over your own soul that you not be taken. If your religion tells you that you are going to hell if you do not belong to their religion, then you are listening to another gospel. And My Word definitely curses any other gospel. The war she saw was a war for the pulpit. One side would not and did not have the Word; therefore, they did not *live* the Word. They only claimed it. The other side wanted the Word but did not know how to obey the Word. I tell you even now the truth, many of you do not know how to obey the Word because you never go into the Word.

The Antichrist will come in his own name. He will be a great communicator. He will seem to bring so much peace and hope, and many will look upon him as a savior. His ability to speak to all nations will be phenomenal. You know why he will have this power? Because he is not of me, and neither are many other nations. The world loves its own. He will seem to have the answer to many problems, be able to speak to all others in other nations that have always hated and distrusted the West. And he will seemingly become all things to all men so that he can accomplish his will, to his purpose, to his agenda. At first he will appear very righteous, and what knowledge he has in that righteousness will appear very genuine because he really doesn't know. Inside of his heart, he will never reveal who he really is. He will seem to be a Christian. He will seem to have some righteousness or at least the ability to reach out to God.

Hitler had this kind of power to persuade so many people, to sweep across his nation and convince them to destroy the Jews. The worst atrocities were committed because destroying another human being was so easily accepted. He had no respect or honor for the elderly. He rose up an army of young people because *the young are easy to deceive because they do not have the knowledge that can only be obtained by experience.* Listen carefully to what I say, because for a long time, it will not be seen until it is time to manifest. Just as Judas went to sup with Jesus and dipped his bread, so shall this man. And by the time you see him manifest, it may be too late. This will be something that will never be revealed until the time. It can only be seen by God's children who are filled with the Holy Spirit, filled with the Word of God Jesus, and filled with My will. The world right now is ripe to worship anyone. You can see it in the young, how they worship at their concerts, how people worship celebrities. He will have been with Jesus long enough to have learned how to handle himself and how to say all the right things in order to appear to be what he is not. And then suddenly he will turn. Whether he is on the earth today is unimportant because it will only come to pass when it is time. It will never be seen until that moment that I choose to manifest it.

Remember that Judas did not do one thing until the time appointed. Picture the scene in your mind. He kept silent as he walked and talked with Jesus and His disciples. He never revealed what was truly working within him. Do not deceive yourself into thinking that anyone knew until the moment that it happened. This is why My Word says that they asked, "Is it I, Lord?" Judas's closest associates did not know until the moment. This is why no one right now knows the time or the hour all these things will happen. Many of you will not understand what I am saying here, but all who are Mine will. And many of you will be tempted to believe even now that you see him, here or there. I tell you *I have not revealed him yet,* and I will reveal him to Mine, not all of you who claim to be Mine are Mine. You must have the Word abiding in you to be Mine. Many of you think because you are with Me you are entitled to know ahead of time, but this is not according to My Word. The son of perdition is the only one appointed to be lost. Listen to what I Am saying and ponder on the truth of these Words.

His persuasion will be very powerful; at first it will seem as though I Am with him because of his ability to persuade through speech. The only way you will know him is by examining his fruits and never by his words. I have told you many times that there are many Antichrists in the world, so do not deceive yourselves into believing that you know who I Am speaking about. I will let you know in the appointed time.

PART V

"And when He was demanded of the Pharisees, when the kingdom of God should come, He answered them and said, *The kingdom of God cometh not with observation:* Neither shall they say, Lo here! Or, lo there! For, behold the kingdom of God is within you. And he said unto the disciples, 'The days will come, when ye shall desire to see one of the days of the Son of man, and ye shall not see it.' And they shall say to you, See here; or, see there: go not after them, nor follow them. *For as the lightning, that lighteneth out of the one part under heaven, shineth unto the other part under heaven; so shall also the Son of man be in His day*" (Luke 17:20-24 KJV).

The words in this book are the words that will enlighten you to get ready for the rapture. They are what I want revealed, for the time is at hand to be ready, and if I do not deal with you here, you will never be ready to go with Jesus. Take a look at this scripture, ask yourself why would I say that they shall say see here or see there? Why would I tell you go not after them? *The kingdom of God is within you.* Why do you run everywhere to find Him? He is right there in your home, with you in the Word, with you in the Spirit. Why do you run everywhere to find Him? You need healing, He is within you. You need deliverance, He is within you. I will tell you why, because you have not

64

done what you are supposed to do according to My Word to allow the kingdom of God to prosper within you.

Just consider this: I will not come in the wind, I will not come in the rain, and I will not come in the snow, for I need nothing within the earth to deal with you. I will not come in another person. I will not come in a storm; I most definitely will come within the temple that you dwell in. I will come within you. The terror will be within a man's soul and a place where only he knows exists, but more importantly a place where only I know all things. In your very being, you will feel it. Where you have played with My words, where you have played with all of life and souls, I will most definitely visit within you. Those who are obedient and have come to ask Me if they are where they need to be, and My Presence confirmed it shall be very blessed for them in that day.

I am going to visit everyone within himself or herself. Listen to what I say! I am not saying that I am going to take your physical life. What I Am saying is that I Am going to deal with you and lead you to repentance because I love you. This is so important, for it is time that you get off of the milk of the word and begin to eat the meat. Trusting in Me for a new car or a new anything is feeding off of the milk. The visit will come from within, the way I came to her from within. My Glory is going to sweep your minds, your hearts, and your bodies and overwhelm you to the point that the flesh will not be able to endure it unless you have the baptism of the Holy Spirit. Everyone receives the Holy Spirit at conversion. My Spirit leads and directs you and reveals all the truth about Jesus that you need. In spite of the fact that you turn Me off, you reject Me, and you go on your own way, and all the while you claim to be going My way. And I continually work and labor with you. Matthew 3:8-12 (KJV) says, "Bring forth therefore fruits meet for repentance: And think not to say within yourselves, we have Abraham to our father: for I say unto you, that God is able of these stones to raise up children unto Abraham. And now also the axe is laid unto the root of the trees: therefore every tree which bringeth not forth good fruit is hewn down, and cast into the fire. I indeed baptize you with water unto repentance: but he that cometh after Me is mightier than I, whose shoes I am not worthy to bear: He shall baptize you with the Holy Ghost, and with fire: Whose fan is in His hand, and He will thoroughly purge His floor, and gather His wheat into the garner; but He will burn up the chaff with unquenchable fire."

At times I have put within you a love for My son, which is the Word, My Spirit, the church, and all others. And this has been only at times according to how much you have permitted Me to dwell within you. This is why sometimes you don't feel as though you love anyone or are able to think of anyone outside yourself. You have not lined up to Me or to My instruction book. *The touches of My Spirit that you receive even in worship are to get you going in the right direction. They are to lead you into all truth. Not to use as though you have already attained anything.* Every time I ever visited anyone in the Spirit even with the smallest touch with My Presence was to cause them to want so much more that they would seek Me more in the Word. And many times these touches were taken so for granted as though you deserved to be blessed if you did any little thing that I had required of you. It was and is all your reasonable service. Yet you took it for granted, took it as though I owed it to you, and took it so lightly that you simply continued on your way without Me. I Am not speaking to all of you, for there are many who truly love Me enough to worship Me with their lives by living and breathing My Word, and when they get touched, it is a confirmation of My pleasure in them.

At those moments that you are doing My will, according to My Word in agreement and accordance with My Spirit, you can feel My Presence. And many, many times you will find yourself wondering why I don't seem to be with you at all times. I am only with you to the degree that you allow Me. I am only present according to the amount that you allow Me to be. You tie My hands, and I cannot witness even to you that you are in My will when in moments, hear me, moments you turn your own way more times than not. And what do you do during these times? You continue as though you have not left Me. Why? Ask yourself why. Why do you not then get on your knees and repent and seek to be with Me always in everything? I will reveal to you why right now. You do not want to. You live in the flesh, and you refuse to come when I call, and you expect Me to do it all for you. You have the Holy Spirit, and because you do, you dishonor that fact by expecting Me to do it all for you. All the while in this disobedience to My Spirit, you claim and believe that you are somehow going to be all right. Please work it out with Me. Talk to Me about it so that I can direct you in how to permit Me to dwell within you forever. It is a growing of faith, a growth that begins with the realization that no, it will not be all right until you get it right. Then you can have the relationship you so desire with Me. Until that day that you let Me in, what can I do? Can you not see that I will never go against the truth of My word and even though some of you may dishonor My Son, I will not?

I wrote this book with a simple message, "Let Me in!" I will not force you, but I will give you all the chances in the world to receive the truth if you claim Me. That claim gives Me the right to help you. Don't be deceived when you ask Me to come in and be your Lord. *I do just that, I come in.* Are you so foolish that you do not know what those words mean? A Lord rules and controls your life from the moment you ask. He isn't a leader; He is a King that rules. He doesn't ask if you want to obey, He commands that you do. What happens if someone disobeys a king here on earth? Do they get to give their side of it? His kingdom is not a democracy where you have a say. He rules and reigns. If you displease Me, I have a right to do whatsoever I choose with you. I have the right to correct you, to even stop you if I see that you are determined to do evil in My kingdom. What I say goes. You asked My Son King Jesus to come into your heart, and He will not rule in unrighteousness. But He will rule according to His Word, according to His righteousness; and if you deliberately go against that, you then are asking for trouble. Make yourself safe and be sure. Because you refuse to see it the way it is; because you did not take the time or the effort to understand your commitment. Because you did not take the time or the effort to understand what all of that meant doesn't stop the reality of the fact that He is King, He is Lord, and He will rule and reign because you asked Him to. He doesn't leave you, but you do leave Him.

Some say that My Spirit is a perfect gentleman, and I will never force you to do anything. It is true that I will never force any man to love Me, to serve Me, to love their neighbor, or to do what is right. *But once I come by your invitation, all things change.* I then have been given power over you. I created you for Me. I Am not created for you. I longed to have someone who would love Me that has a free choice to do so. I have no interest in someone who doesn't want Me. Ask yourself a question. If you loved someone who disrespected you, who never wanted anything to do with you or worse yet neglected and ignored you, would you put up with it, or would you do something about it? You can't captivate Me with the way that you are or the way you captivate others. You can't cause Me to believe anything, feel anything, and decide anything without Jesus Christ. He gave so much for you that *I demand* everyone who hears of Him to make a choice. *I demand respect and honor toward Him.* This means that you must have respect and honor for the Word because in John 1:1 I tell you all plainly that *Jesus is the Word.* And if you never read the word or study the word or ponder and meditate on the word, then how can you have Him come within you? You are rejecting Him as you claim Him. You put Him on a shelf, and you go to a church that takes a tiny piece of the gospel and reads it as though it is holy and unobtainable, and you live your life under your strength, seemingly, which will fail you, under your guidance which will misdirect you. Or you let some other man who claims to be holy or greater than you or even another woman to advise you. And never does it occur to you that My Word is alive, and it is the Living Word. Once you put it into your hearts and minds and you keep it there by faith, then and only then are you serving the Living God, and you then let the Living Word work within you. And I will then rule.

Yes, my love is unconditional. An unconditional love for someone else is never based on how you are treated, how you are talked to. It remains no matter what. This love stands steady, never wavering, never moving from its original position. You love them. They do sometimes painful and terrible things, and you still love them. This is how I feel. My love holds steady no matter what is said, what is done. That is unconditional. That unconditional love was given when you accepted Jesus. *To continue in the faith is no longer unconditional. You now have to do your part.* Because I love you, it doesn't mean that I will not correct you, nor does it mean that I will not deal with you. And I plainly wrote it in the Word that I will not always strive with you. Knowing that you are but a mortal who will one day leave this earth, I strive with you to bring you to a place of complete repentance. Knowing your time is so short. Knowing that the next moment could be your last breath, I strive to guide and direct you into all truth. That is unconditional love. But in Romans chapter 1, I describe it plainly. That when you do not like to retain God in your knowledge, when you change the image of who I Am into something like who you are, when you take My Glory and glorify man, then I give you up to what you want. I let you go because I revealed through all that I made My righteousness and holiness. Because you never took the time to ponder it, to understand it, to meditate on it, and then you toss it aside like it is simply some sort of garbage, and you do that continually, how do you expect Me to continue to work to get someone in, who doesn't want in even as they say they do want in? *The whole time you don't want it, you still claim it. I call that crazy!*

When you are young and unaware of certain things, I seem to sometimes wink at those things you do especially if I know that you are striving to serve Me. But after I have given you warning after warning, year after year, and you still insist on things your way, what would you do if you were Me? I know that you ask what Jesus would do. But I ask you that if you were God, what would you do? I know what My Word says I will do. I will require the truth of the Word to live and exist in every man who claims to be Mine. I will require for him to accept his responsibility, to take up his cross and follow Me. People do not read the Word because of the conviction in it. They do not want to hear that I will give you houses and lands that you did not buy *with persecutions.* They do not want to read *deny yourself and follow thou Me.* Many will tell you that they do not want to suffer. And I assure you that life is so that you will suffer and endure, and it might as well have a reward in Jesus. How foolish that some of you are striving to escape responsibility to the Word.

Paul the Apostle knew what he was talking about when he said, "Knowing the terror of the Lord, we persuade all men." From the moment of our first encounter, he knew he was no longer contending with man. For the vessel who wrote this book, from the moment of our first encounter, she knew that she no longer was contending with man. Of all the things that Paul suffered, he was not afraid of anything.

Bitten by a snake, he simply brushed it off knowing it was poisonous and could not harm him. Paul wasn't afraid in prison; he was delivered. He wasn't afraid in all the perilous things that he endured. But he shook and trembled before Me when I visited him within his own soul. His body was filled with terror, which I revealed to him My Glory, and he wondered within himself why he wasn't dead. This is how and why he could endure so many things so faithfully, so powerfully, because he knew the terror of the Lord. He knew no other desire or fear but Mine.

The fear of the Lord is the beginning of wisdom, and without it you can face a hopeless place, thinking that it is all right or it is going to be all right and you can gloss it over or cover yourself with a covering that is not of Me. You can justify your actions and words and make something that isn't sin a sin simply because you think you have gotten one over on Me.

I am not talking to you about you having a touch of the Holy Spirit. You can be touched and be blessed and feel My presence and still not be where I want you to be. You can be anointed to preach or teach and still not be where I want you. And as long as you are not where I want you, you take a chance of not ever getting there. Read the Word, salvation can be lost. You can refuse My call and reject My Spirit, tramp on My Son's blood, and fall. The only way you are safe and your sins are not imputed is when you have all of your sins under the blood of My Son Jesus Christ and are with all of your heart laboring with Me to be what I want you to be. The only path to that labor is forgiveness and repentance. And once I reveal to you through a word like this that you are not where you need to be, and you do not repent, then you can have trouble. I want you blessed; I want you safe, so all the things written in this book are for your safety. It is better for you to come before me and examine yourself than to take the chance of leaving something undone. I say these things for your sakes, not Mine.

I desire to make all of this very plain in speech that I Am not speaking to the sinner or the one who knows nothing about Me. I Am not speaking to anyone who never reads the Bible or who doesn't even want to read the Bible. I Am not speaking to those who do not claim to know, have, or understand everything. I Am speaking to people who claim to have Me in their heart and do not!

PART VI

"Love *suffereth long*, and *is kind*; love *envieth not*; love *vaunteth not itself*, *is not puffed up*, *doth not behave itself unseemly*, *seeketh not her own*, *is not easily provoked*, *thinketh no evil*; *rejoiceth not in iniquity*, *but rejoiceth in the truth*; *beareth all things*, *believeth all things*, *hopeth all things*, *endureth all things*. Love *never faileth*: but whether there be prophecies, they shall fail; whether there be tongues, they shall cease; whether there be knowledge, it shall vanish away" (1 Corinthians 13:4-8).

Whatever happened to the "I can do all things through Christ who strengthens me"? Not the attitude that "I can't bear it, I can't take it," or flying off the handle every time you encounter something that doesn't please your flesh. That is what it is you know, the flesh. It rules and reigns. Have you ever read James? When you strive and war, there is confusion and every evil work. And like all men or women, it is always everyone else's fault. It is so much easier to never deal with yourself.

This vessel that wrote this has been married for going on forty-five years. Hard roads taught her to back up and restore the things that she took not away. Lest at any time the ministry be blamed. Whose will do you follow, yours or Mine? Psalm 69:3, 4 (KJV) says, "I am weary of

71

my crying: my throat is dried: mine eyes fail while I wait for my God. They that hate me without a cause are more than the hairs of mine head: they that would destroy me, being mine enemies wrongfully, are mighty: *then I restored that which I took not away."*

I Am not telling you anything about her spouse except that he has learned also how to be good to her and respect her, and he always did a good job of taking care of her. But many times she did not think so. And many times I had to talk to her and remind her of how he took care of her. When you're young, it never occurs to you that the person you have chosen to spend your life with may become sick and need you. It never occurs to you that perhaps your looks fade; if that is what you built your relationship on, then your relationship will fade. It never enters your mind that one day you will be getting older and you will be needing someone to be with you and choose to love you enough to take care of you. Do you cut off the other half of you simply because your flesh is no longer pleased? Perhaps they don't seem to be whom you married. Give more love and I can promise you that you will receive more love. Look not on your desires or needs but on the fact that the one you chose doesn't have the ability to grasp hold of the love of Me that you are so blessed with. And that perhaps you are the only one that I can use to love them enough to see My love in you. Many times this vessel fell to her knees with the heart broken because her spouse did not have the love and comfort that *he* needed in My Son. Where is your compassion? How far does it take you to understand how My love works? A good man or woman is hard to find, and some of you desire a good man or a good woman, and yet you do not realize that if you had one in your present condition of mind, you would help to destroy them. I Am not telling you to put up with abuse or beatings. I Am telling you to take a good look in the mirror. Sit down and see if your other half has good things about them that outweigh the bad. For what seems bad may be your own selfish desires. Write down all the good things and all the things that hurt and upset you, and you may find out that the good outweighs the bad.

Take this message as one delivered directly from My Throne. Take it as an encouragement that although you have done so many things against Me, it is never too late to turn away from it. And believe that the power of the blood of Jesus Christ is so powerful that it will deliver you and heal your spirit. For the Spirit within you that is fully Mine cannot commit such sins. A spirit within you that is fully Mine cannot bring forth such evil fruit. Let Me change you, heal you, and deliver you. For once you turn against Me, you become guilty. How did you turn against Me, you say? When I called you to holiness, perfection in heart, by putting the Word in you, you did not answer but answered the call of the world, the flesh, and the devil. I want you, to cleanse you and bring you to the heavenly places that I called you to, not to the ones that you claim you are in. In 1 John 1:4-10 (KJV), it says, "And these things write we unto you, that your joy may be full. This then is the message which we have heard of Him, and declare unto you, *that God is light and in Him is no darkness at all*. If we say that we have fellowship with him, and walk in darkness, we lie, and do not the truth: but if we walk in the light, as He is in the light, we have fellowship one with another and the blood of Jesus Christ His Son cleanseth us from all sin. If we say that we have no sin, we deceive ourselves, and the truth is not in us. If we confess our sins, He is faithful and just to forgive us our sins and to cleanse us from all unrighteousness. If we say that we have not sinned, we make Him a liar, and His Word is not in us."

Take this journey with Me, and let Me lead you to a place that will reveal to you every place that you turned your back on Me. If you are not doing My will, then that disobedience withholds all that I have for you. You search and search and search, you believe and believe and believe, and you speak My word and speak My word and speak My word. And some of you have done this for many, many years waiting for a promise that I cannot come and answer because you never truly came to Me to begin with. This is not a one-time visit at the altar. This isn't something that your pastor can help you pray your way through. This is something that has to be worked out daily by you and Me to develop a long-lasting relationship with Me. You don't wave a magic wand or say some magic-working words and then suddenly change. *You work daily and work it out with Me in everything.* And while you do that, I can and will work on the rest of your life. Up until now, you have used Me and

My Word to suit yourself in such a way that you fully expect to have everything when you do a minimum.

I had such great plans for you, and up until now you have done nothing but manipulate your knowledge of Me to suit yourself. You sit in a church, and some of you are so wrapped up in your ministry or calling or your supposedly close walk with Me that everyone dies around you. Watching you care only for yourselves has required much patience on My part. I have been very long-suffering with you. But the day that is here is a day of forgiveness and repentance and making things within your life truly new. When you turn the light off and do your own thing, the darkness is greater than the one who turns openly away and continues in their own way in deep sin. For your thinking is like the alcoholic that drinks only beer, they have so many reasons to say that they are not alcoholics even though it destroys their relationships with their spouses and children. Even though it corrupts their minds to believe that right is wrong and wrong is right. Even though daily their brains are eaten away and their lives are lived in oblivion. Until there is no way, no hope, and all they have and all they own are destroyed. One day, all too late, they waken up as to what they are; and they walk in this life now worse than before if they cannot see that they have spent years running away from life, years running away from the truth, years living a life on a barstool, perhaps avoiding the responsibilities of life and the very basics that they owe to themselves, to their spouses, to their homes, to their families, and to their fellow men and their country as a citizen. And they have no clue as to how to make it right. And when they do not seek help in My Word, they become worse than before because now they do all the things that they used to do, they walk in all the ways as they used to walk, they think exactly the way they used to think except for one thing: now they are sober and have no excuse. They have now become a dry drunk. They think, act, feel, and function according to all the years they spent on a barstool; and life and living passed them by as the brain slowly got eaten up. Now they come to God and use the same mind-set. Only now with the Word, they corrupt themselves even more. Why? They receive not the love of the truth. Their pride rules them still for something that makes sense to them, and because they never wanted to do it My way, they turn to doctrines that destroy them all over again. All because they refuse to go into My Word and repent down to the last deed, to the last word, until it is all finished and worked out with fear and trembling before Me. I Am not speaking of all alcoholics that drank beer. I Am not speaking of any one particular person. I Am speaking to those who know to do good and doeth it not; to them it is a sin. I Am speaking to those who believe all they have to do is shut things out of their mind. Those who do not understand that no matter what you bury and no matter how deep you bury it and for how long you seem to succeed, you must give it to Me. Come and talk to Me about it. Not your neighbor who cannot help you with this burden. But the One who promised to lift any and all burdens. If you do not release it to Me and cry on your knees, in a godly sorrow for the places you failed. Or for all the times you strove within yourself to do it yourself. That is a tremendous, terrible burden, and there is only one release, and that is to bring it to the altar of prayer and give it all to Me whether you chose to pray at your altar in your home or in a church. I will in no wise cast you out. When you come to Me, you are then safe. As you continue in the faith, we work it out *together*.

But for some of you, oh yes, poor things come and hold their hand. You who do this, who comfort people in their sin, do not realize how you keep that soul lost and entangled, and because unconfessed sin will still follow them to the Judgment, you have made yourselves responsible for another, and every person will stand before Me alone. You have family members that have done things they ought not, and instead of defending Me and the truth, you defend them in their present condition, and they are unable to seek help because they have your support. As a matter of fact, you defend them to the grave. Never considering that the people they hurt needed someone to say that it just wasn't right. But no, you lift those who have done wickedness up so high that you hate people to ever bring the truth out. Is there not even a little of basic understanding of the truth? Can't any of you see that for years before they became addicted, for years they chose to drink above their families? They had to say for years, "I want this, and I don't care what happens to my babies, I don't care what happens to the spouse, I don't care what happens to my job, I don't care that I am robbing them of their lives, their finances, and even their work for they paid me a wage and I was never sober to do the job correctly." "I cheated everybody" is what their cry needs to be. And if they never cry it, I can't forgive them. Because I promised in My word that unconfessed sin will still follow them to the judgment. If they refuse to believe that they are responsible and they continue to deny that they have to humble themselves and admit the things they did and ask for forgiveness. When it is easier to go to a place in their brain that says somehow, someway it will all be all right. Not so. It is according to my Word only. Haven't you read in Matthew that if your brother has ought against you, you first go to them and make it right with them and then offer your gift to Me? Matthew 5:23, 24 (KJV) says, "Therefore if thou bring thy gift to the altar, and there rememberest that thy brother hath ought against thee; Leave there thy gift before the altar, and go thy way; first be reconciled to thy brother, and then come and offer thy gift." Are you so blind that you cannot see that your gift is giving your life to Me? Are you so foolish as to believe that I will accept that gift from someone who has hurt so many others for years and then you say one prayer and never face the consequences or the responsibility to others, that somehow I will just wipe it all clean without you doing your part of the covenant? Can't you see that I made it so that you must humble your heart and ask for forgiveness from someone else? Otherwise, you will remain in a continual state of denial until you fool yourself so much for so long that you shut the only door to Me. The only "way" I made for man was to humble himself before a Living God and ask for forgiveness and humble himself before those that he owes a debt to. Do you not realize that I cannot cancel your debts until you cancel the debt that you owe to others? Read it in Matthew, how I forgave a man for all the things he had done simply because he begged me to forgive him. Then he went and refused to forgive someone for the things that were done to him. Oh, I see, some of you are so high, so self-deceived, so proud that you don't need to read the Word. Oh, but you do need to read it every day to strengthen the things of God within you and most of all so that you don't lose them.

In the middle of the night, sometimes you wake up and become afraid of dying. Now why do you suppose you are doing that? You have to push and shove everything out of your mind that tells you that something is wrong. You are pushing and shoving Me. You are striving against My conviction power sent through the presence of My Holy Spirit to enlighten you to the truth that can set you free. I Am striving to reveal to you that you need to forget all of your pride and ask for forgiveness from everyone that you hurt. This isn't a matter of going on doing what you think I said, but it is a matter of doing things My way. I am the Way, the Truth, and the Life. It is My Way, not yours. John 14:6 (KJV) says, "Jesus saith unto him, I am the Way, the Truth, and the Life: no man cometh unto the Father, but by Me."

Some of you that have come out of drugs, alcohol, or any kind of addiction do not realize that it was a self-centered thinking, a giving in to always to self, a way of escaping any and all realities and responsibilities. And you carry this with you into what you think is a new relationship with Christ. All of your thoughts and feelings center on you as you get into the Word. This is why you apply everything negative to others and only positive to yourself. You are as blind as you were when you turned away from what you were doing in some ways. And the same spirit that led you to drink now leads you to believe that I Am with you when you misapply My Word to suit yourself and never consider others. I know that what I Am saying right now seems impossible, but I Am telling you the truth. That until you get rid of any kind of self-centered thinking and feelings, you cannot and will not ever learn how to be in My will. Do not let it hinder you. Every person knows within themselves when they have compassion, when they are motivated through compassion. And if you do not check your motivations, you can do some of the best acts and they still can center from self. A check on your heart should be often in asking Me to reveal to you if there is anything in you that is not of Me. I will be right there, and I promise you that if I reveal to you a problem, I only reveal it to you to take it away through the blood. I do not ever reveal these things to My children to demand them to cry or be so sorry that they cannot get up. I reveal it so that it can be confessed, repented of, and to learn of Me. Some of you can't see that you are in this condition. Please help Me to help you to make it all right. Come to Me about all the things written in this book, just as every man should come to Me about everything written in My word. The Bible is a mirror; as you open it up, you can see your own reflection as to *exactly* who you are. You see where you have obeyed and where you have not. It is to be used to lead you into all truth; this is a guide to help you get into the guide the way you ought to. And see yourselves as you are, not as you think you are. That you may be what I desire you to be, not as you think I desire you to be. You wonder why I seem to be preaching to the choir, and that is because some of you sing, but a lot of you don't live within Me.

Some of you have suffered a lot of things. And because you have suffered or endured these things, you are so foolish as to believe that you are a prophet. My prophets don't become prophets because they suffered or endured anything. This prophet suffered and endured because she was and is a prophet. The enemy strove to destroy her so that this message and others would never come forth. It took her about thirty-five to thirty-eight years to perfect the gift as a prophet to be able to hear My voice in all these things to deliver this message to you.

Those of you who are gifted with prophetic utterances and have no understanding for how I operate within the mind and heart of every vessel, you need to take special heed to this message. Those of you who know the word through knowledge have no idea of what I am speaking of. Those of you who have had Me to back up your utterances and prove them to be true were mouthpieces for Me. And there are those of you who to this day take from other prophets, other preachers, and make it look like I am speaking through you because you are some great one who knows everything. You get your so-called fresh revelation from others, not from Me. This vessel did not take what anyone said or what anyone taught. She took it directly from Me, striving with every atom of her being to be sure that the flesh could not touch one place within her to corrupt the message that I want for this hour. And some of you out there have part of this message. Whatever she lacks, you will fit like a puzzle that fits tightly together, for I most definitely do have prophets in the church. But I also have those who only think they have something, and it is to those I am speaking these words of warning.

You need to understand that it is not the things she suffered or endured that she has this calling. It is not anything about her except that I chose her. Some of you are going to hate her and desire to destroy her, and I will tell you now that even if this is a path that you choose to take, this will not affect her one bit. It will not touch her. But it will affect and touch you unless you repent. For I have lifted her up high, high above those who think that they can judge her or anyone like her; and as long as I chose her, no weapon formed against her shall prosper. I preplanned for her to be able to endure any and all harsh words against her. It was all part of her training to bring her to the place that none of it from anybody can or will touch her. I will let no man judge her. Listen to what I am saying. There is a reason for all of this. That reason goes further than what you can imagine. Understand this, for I am going to be very clear in speech. When you think you see inside of her heart or her mind as a prophet, when you think that I would give you anything about her personal heart or mind concerning anything, when you are sure that you can see her and understand her in the Spirit, when you are positive that I would give that to you, remember this: I have not, and she feels it, sees it, and knows it; and just as I led Jesus through a crowd that wanted to stone Him, I led her right out of your hands. And you will be found to have nothing within your hands. Now this statement you can take and apply to yourself for protection, but I promise you that if I Am not with you on it, none of it in the end will do you any good to take one thing she teaches or preaches to claim it for your own. To have what she has, you *must have Me*; and I promise you, I will not call an imitator, a copycat, or a pretender. For she is Mine! And the price she paid to be able to speak to prophets was too high for any one of you to be able to make her what you think. Be sure of one thing, that when you think you have any answers concerning her, you cannot and will not ever find Me out. For no man will ever tell Me what to do with what is Mine. And even though for years I have been with you, and even though for years you seemed to be right on the money, I warn you today that I called this prophet to a purpose and a very special task and

79

no one will take that away from her. So when you believe that you know better than her, understand I Am with her. And when you think that I Am with you, understand that unless you paid a great price to obtain such a calling, you may find yourself having to pay what she paid. There is a price to all of your callings. And you need to understand this is a prophet that I called for this hour. And I tell you plainly that no man, no woman would ever want to go down the path that she has gone.

Those of you who prophesy what is in a man's heart *must be sure* that God revealed the good or the bad. It is very important during this hour that you receive directly from the Holy Spirit. I say this for a reason because some have a surface gift, and one that operates on the surface for they have never yielded to Me to go any further in understanding. You could call it shallow if you want to. But only a part of their heart is very shallow. There are those who have been anointed to see the truth as something tangible coming to them through experience. When I say anointed, I do not mean seeming to try the spirits on the surface of understanding. I mean from knowing Me so well, knowing Me so closely through living the Word of God you have no shadow of turning in your hearts. If your prophetic words are surface, you will see according to that surface, and because it has not enough understanding through experience of endurance with Me, you can and will be deceived, for even the very elect will be deceived if it were possible. Mark 13:22 (KJV) says, "For false Christ's and false prophets shall rise, and shall show signs and wonders, to seduce, if it were possible, even the elect."

PART VII

"But Jesus did not commit himself unto them, because he knew all men" (John 2:24 KJV).

Now if Jesus did not commit Himself to any man, how can we speak for any man? We can say that God revealed to us for whatever purpose to support this one or that. But we can never say what is within their hearts is good or bad. When a man or a woman is *ungodly in their choices* and they claim to be Mine and I reveal to you that they *could* win an office, it is for you to pray for them *not* to obtain anything without repenting. This is where the prayers of the prophets come in. A prophet doesn't go along with the sin and feed it in power by believing and confessing that they see something good in someone who will do something that I never will put my stamp of approval on. Do you realize that if I Am not with sin, I Am not with sin? That doesn't mean I hate the person, but why as a prophet would I give you a message that goes directly against My Word to fulfill? All men that we meet and have contact with that have even a shallow relationship with Christ do have an ability of righteousness within them. That is no reason that I should stand and support them in their endeavors unless those endeavors are in pure works of the gospel. I stand with no particular man against any other particular man. I will not go to a prophet and speak for them or against them because I know how all men work. But what I will do is once a person is in office, I will be there to lead, guide, and direct them if they permit Me. If a person believes and stands for something that is against My Word, then how can I lead, guide, and direct them? Because they make a confession that they belong to Me or love My Son is not enough. Their fruits must bear witness. *Your fruits are not what you say, they are what you do.* They are not what you promise to do, but what you have already done and achieved thus far.

Why would any of you want to put your relationship with Me in jeopardy because someone sounds good? I don't hate people who love one another of the same gender. I do not willfully and deliberately work to hurt them. But the consequences of their choices are against them, and if and when you strive to make things easy for them, where are you when you claim to be Mine? Consequences for their actions were designed by Me to lead them to repentance, not make a way for them to be comforted in their sins.

Where is your wisdom? If someone you love, for instance, your child, decides to do something that you know is not good for them, and it will bring consequences upon them that will hurt them for years to come, do you make it easier for them to do it or continue in it? Or do you as a responsible parent let them learn for themselves how wrong it is? And if you continue to be their savior out of every problem, how then do you ever help them to learn what to do or not to do? But some of you are concerned only about power and money.

More than most of you know or understand, any office in this country has been anointed by Me. It takes the Holy Spirit to be a good mother, a good father, a good son, a good sibling, a good soldier, a good citizen, etc. The only way that the Holy Spirit can accomplish what any of you have been assigned to do in life is for you to permit the Word of God to abide so completely within a reality of "living" that the flesh cannot creep in and deceive you. In your thinking, if you do not stand for God and you stand for any man during this hour, then it will be like this for you: one day you know what you are doing and the next day it can change and the only way you can come back to where I want you to be is to be humble enough to hear My voice that you may have made a mistake. But I assure you that if you do not seek My Presence on everything that you say and do in leadership, you can and will be found to be mistaken. You say that is impossible? Then I say you should have labored to do this so long ago or even first. For all those who are sincerely Mine have already done such a work. I Am not speaking about you suffering. I Am speaking about you being in a position that no matter how many followers you have, they will actually see you are not where you claim to be. For of My prophets I demand complete obedience, not partial. I demand complete love, not partial, for Me to use you for My Glory. What has transpired up until now will not be enough.

Everyone must now get on their knees and pray. I Am not speaking of praying against your brother and demanding them not to succeed in something that you don't want them to have. I Am speaking of praying for My will, and My will alone. Not corrupted by your flesh or your will. The hour that is upon you is critical and crucial for My will to be accomplished. And all the playing with the things of God will be cleansed out of the church. As some of My prophets have warned that what is coming for the Christian will be hard to endure but it will be so good for them. You must remember that what I tell one prophet I will tell others to confirm one another.

My church must come together now. I am not speaking of the way the world comes together as you well know. Those who do not have the Spirit are not what I am talking about, nor are they to whom I am speaking. This day in the church has to be lived one day at a time while it is called today. It is a time to get all things right with Me. It is a time to pray that you be found worthy. As I told you before, those with whom I have given much, I will require much. Do not misinterpret or try to interpret what these words mean. These words mean exactly what I Am saying. Those of you who do know Me and have seen My works and My miracles will understand exactly what I Am saying. Those of you who have kept yourself close to Me will understand exactly what this means because I will reveal it to you as you hear these words. No one is greater than the other; no one is higher than the other no matter what your gift is or how I have used you.

Some of you have read this book as a manuscript before it was edited, before it was published, and do not like what you have read. Some of you are so comfortable in where you are at and with what you are doing that it actually irritated you, and that irritation caused you to reject this book. For some of you, it has been something that put sorrow in your heart because it is not yet revealed what is taking place. There is no reason for sorrow, there is no reason for disappointment, and there is no reason to be concerned or upset. I understand that you do not want the light necessarily turned on concerning what seems to be your ministry. And you have every right to be concerned. But this vessel is doing exactly as I called her to do. If you had anything against it, you should have told her because that is why she sent you a copy of her manuscript. She stood before Me more than willing to accept any and all criticism, any and all correction. She has a tremendous respect for all those who are Mine, let alone any pastor that is Mine. This is the time that all of your faith for the faithful years that you have served Me will come together. As I have said before, this hour to you may last ten years and it may last ten days. For the time is all in My hands. There is much to be done, much to pray about. In Christ there is no man, there is no woman; so if that is true and My Word is true, then there is no color. What I write in this book, if a person of a different ethnic group seems to fit the description, I can only say that it is not directed at any one person.

It is directed to anyone and everyone who does the things that I will bring up and bring forth into the light. For what makes manifest is light. And Jesus is the Light of the World, and in Him is no darkness at all. Ephesians 5:13 (KJV) says, "But all things that are reproved are made manifest by the light: for whatsoever doth make manifest is light." When the manuscript was sent whatever hit home with you, if you prayed to take care of it, then it will not appear in this book. There are prophets that I do warn here, and now these prophets do not live in this country, nor were they born here. I call them as a prophet to *their country*; I call prophets to the country that they were born into. Because unless you were born in a country, you really know nothing about it; why would I give you the truth about anything in this country, and what right do you have to claim that I would not give it to My own in their country? You need to keep your hands on what belongs to you. Stay within the calling that you are called.

Some of you will be outraged for a season, and some of you will be envious for a season, and some of you will be very jealous for a season. The truth has a certain amount of offense to it even if it is given in love. The truth is something that at times will hurt in order for it to be effective when the time comes for a need of correction or setting things in proper order. But you must remember that the Word says that you are tempted by "your own lust." It will not be Me who tempts you as I have written in James: "Let no man say when he is tempted, I am tempted of God: for God cannot be tempted with evil, neither tempteth He any man: But every man is tempted, when he is drawn away of his own lust, and enticed. Then when lust hath conceived, it bringeth forth sin: and sin, when it is finished it bringeth forth death. Do not err my beloved brethren" (James 1:13-16 KJV). It will not be the devil who tempts you. But the temptation will *come from within you,* giving you an opportunity to bring every thought into captivity of Christ. This is not something that will happen to the world. And it is not the world that will tempt you or those who do not know Me. But it will be a temptation of what I personally have given to those whom you esteem to be so much less than you. Neither will it happen in the part of the so-called church that believes that they are something that they are not. There are those of you who have already passed through this. But I want you to see what is in you the way I see it. I want all of My children to be purified; they must come to the place that they can plainly see what works within them. So don't be discouraged, My darlings, for it will pass as you pray. The blood of Jesus Christ will cleanse you and keep you. All through this book, I will warn, I will rebuke, I will exhort, and I will most of all love, a love that goes beyond all your understanding. If you endure it faithfully and keep still and quiet before me without crying like babies and complaining of what you think you suffer, you then will thank Me for the privilege. If you don't puff yourselves up and realize when you pass through it that it makes you nothing except doing what is a reasonable service to Me, I Am telling you now that the day is not far up ahead that there will be those who have not taken heed to the call to the Word and in prayer. And on that day, they will change their minds all too late and be left behind. Because the sweep that I Am speaking about cannot be imitated, and it cannot be prophesied by someone who read this manuscript and picked out of it what they so chose to prophesy. The sweep I Am speaking about can only come through the reality of the Word of God living within you. You can use these words and imitate them and think I gave you a new thing. But I am telling you, get into the Word and pray, for none of what I have written through this vessel will be played with, imitated, or used for self-glory to prove you are something.

Many of you I have blessed for such a long, long time. I promise you that those blessings will not lift during this time. I promise you that every promise that I made to you will continue as always. But there are things that are hidden within the heart that need to be brought out in the open for some of you to see. I know and see things that you cannot know or see, and for you this is My way of keeping you safe until the time I call. Because right *now I am doing a new thing in the church, and it is the beginning of a very old thing of truth*. And some of the old ways of understanding have to be brought to a place where it is made real through experience, and experience is difficult to steal from you. Once you learn from experience certain things, you can never be tempted ever again out of them. To know something that was revealed to you is valuable, to know it by hearing and even obeying what you have never experienced is more valuable, but once you experience it as Jesus did, then it becomes something that can never be erased. Hebrews 5:8, 9 (KJV) says, "Though He were a Son, yet learned He obedience by the things which *He suffered; and being made perfect, He became the author of eternal salvation unto all them that obey him*."

Many of you have an attitude that He went through things so that you do not have to. But this is not what My word says. And this is not something that will happen to everyone. It will only happen with those who have not had to endure certain things that they need training on to help them continue during this hour. You will see that this hour on the church is unlike any other hour, and it is going to take a lot more than any man has ever had.

There are those who have searched by leafing through this manuscript, and they did it for only one purpose, and that is to see what it says against them and how it might be able to hinder them and how they may be able to hinder it. And because you did not value it or read it, you tossed it aside as nothing and your venom and your hatred with the evil of your eye upon the author could not touch her. I revealed it all to her. I do not hold anything back from her. You can gather around her all you want and think in the Spirit that you accomplish something, but I assure you she did not write this book, and this book will speak the truth. In every form you can take to pray or think know this, I personally laugh at it, for her anointing far surpasses it in order to be able to help you. Her prayers for you are not to show you something, to prove you something, nor are they to bring you to any place, and most of all they are not to control you or stop you in your purpose for God. She would not dare touch any of Mine. Those that are Mine or not Mine have never had a prayer of control pass through her lips. She understands exactly how to pray, and she would never endure or suffer anyone manipulating and controlling her; I have brought her even surpassing that. We have it now between her and Me, an ability to commune with her My will, and she talks with Me about what I tell her. But she never prays about what another person is doing. She prays constantly for the blessings of Me to flow in righteousness, holiness, and truth only for My will to be done. If I reveal something to her, she knows it is from Me, she doesn't doubt. She knows that once she writes or speaks, she is free of all things, for she has done My will according to My word. This is why it took her so many years to be able to write these things. All during those years, she was being raised in understanding, raised in knowledge, and, simply put, raised in being able to recognize and know Me instantly and to this purpose. I Am telling you plainly that when I speak to her, she never has to pray for it to come to pass, I Am telling you never. You say how can this be? How can anyone not have to speak to Me? This is the relationship I have with her, and I led her into it, and this relationship cannot be imitated, it cannot be pretended, it cannot even be copied or claimed because it takes Me as God to have it, and I have not decided to give it to everyone. I called her to this for this hour, and I took years to perfect it. This is not something that you or anyone can obtain unless I call you to it. I knew there would be those who would willfully and deliberately destroy her and the work that she put in Me, and so I simply protected her that none can find her out or pull her down. We went to a place that I called her to go, that I have not given to everyone or anyone.

How foolish some of you are that have been raised in a Christian home and have had all of the blessings and have never had to endure certain things, and when one comes along that has not your abilities, you look down on them. You even talk about them as though they are garbage under your feet. Some of them when you quickly dismiss them with your intolerance only needed help. You should have asked Me how you could provide help. Although this may not be true for all of them because some will never learn, there are those who have so little, and they in Me can obtain so much; they must not be tossed aside. I know, you say you don't look down on anybody, but We will see. There are those who can't function the way you are able to. And while you enjoy so much, they struggle so hard. I told you in My Word not to judge according to the eyes, to judge righteous judgment, that you not lift yourself up above where you are. John 7:24 (KJV) says, "Judge not according to the appearance, but judge righteous judgment." Your gift has the ability to corrupt you with pride only because deep within pride is still there in you. Not that there is anything wrong with the gift, but how it is used in the thinking. It is *never* what I say to the prophet; its only corruption is what the prophet says I said. They filter it through the flesh. They filter it through their limited understanding of Me. And so when I speak, they think I said something that I never said.

And they will know we are Christians by our love. If a woman makes a mistake with her body and winds up with a child living and breathing within her, she is not entitled to a choice to be able to keep it or kill it. This is not even love for the mother because unless you are totally given up to the enemy of your soul, you will suffer being sorry you did such a thing. Because if you have any sense of right or wrong, you will feel it, and that is why the world insists on counseling you. To get you to accept that it is okay if you destroy you own child. Some of you think that that precious little human being is a punishment to the woman if she is young and has made a mistake. How can you say you love Me and look at your own grandchild as a punishment?

PART VIII

"And I heard a loud voice saying in heaven, Now is come salvation, and strength, and the kingdom of our God, and the power of His Christ: for the accuser of our brethren is cast down, which accused them before our God day and night. And they *overcame him by the blood of the Lamb and by the word of their testimony; and they loved not their lives unto the death*" (Revelation 12:10, 11 KJV).

If you would have met this vessel years ago when she had so little understanding and a huge mental and emotional problem, you would not have wasted your precious time to help her. Therefore, I personally did take the time, and look at how it paid off. With total and complete trust that I was in control, she yielded to listening to every word that I spoke to her. Nothing could come between us. My hand is mightier than the enemies', and this was and is My will to bring her to this place. You imagine even now as you compare yourself to her that I mean according to the limitation of *your* experience and knowledge. I Am speaking about My speaking to her every morning, noon, and night for two solid years without her *ever* saying one word to Me. I had her plead the blood of Jesus over every single thought that passed through her brain, morning, noon, and night for two more years. And if I were to tell it all to you, you still would not understand because I do not call many like this. And it isn't a matter of someone choosing to copy her because *you would have had to have been her to do it.* I did this within her so that those of you who call yourself a prophet could *never correct her* when I speak through her. For you will see the day that it will be proven that you do not know Me enough to teach, correct, or tell her anything. She is called to do exactly what I say, not you. That I Am able to reach her and help her, and in doing that, I am able to reach and help others. At the end of those early years, I revealed to her that very few people ever open the door to Me and let Me completely in enough to tell all that I think and say about everything that is important to Me. And I loved her for being this way with Me, and oh, how she loved Me and loves Me.

She would live and breathe just to be with Me. She never complained about one soul, and she had many against her, many who spoke about her behind her back. She was always afraid that I would hold it against them, and so she would fall to her knees and scream and scream and scream because of the pain that was so unendurable for any human being. The pain of emotionally being so alone and living every day without any word of encouragement or understanding of any kind. Not a day went by without the enemy running rampant on her home and at the church where no one ever encouraged her. They were literally told that if they were kind to her she would misunderstand it. Even at her home, they told each other the words of kindness had to be withheld or she would misunderstand, when the opposite was true. It was they who misunderstood, and through the spread of lies, she suffered untold emotional pain for a long time. Had I not put My hand upon her, she would have perished forever. *Because of the anointing of the Word,* she overcame it all. Listen to what I say. I did not say because of the anointing of the Holy Spirit which she did and does have. *But the anointing that can only come from knowing Jesus in the Word is what saved her. Jesus saved her! My Spirit brought the Word to her, but the Word itself living within her brought her out victoriously.*

So many of you that knew her thought you suffered and endured as much as her. I tell you now, not so because you refused to live the word as I spoke to your heart. You applied it your way, not Mine. And here is your proof that I lifted her up. Have I lifted you up? Are you lifted out of the poverty of being without understanding? Can you honestly say in all things that I have delivered you? Or are you still in mediocrity, waiting to be uplifted because you refused Me when I spoke the truth? This book is the truth, and if you accept it fully, you may get a little picture of where you are at now and why. *Then* you will have taken your first steps to spiritual freedom. *Where she feared you would endure judgment, you prayed it upon her. Does that give you a clue? Where you worked lies and iniquity of the worst kind and thought that because you were able to seem to succeed you could tell everyone evil about someone like her until it seemed to surround her enough to seem true.* And you now expect Me to lift you. How does that work? Tell Me, how does it work? I Am not speaking to one person. I Am not speaking to one situation, one condition. I Am not writing this to vindicate her, for she is already vindicated. I Am not writing this to defend her, for she is already defended. She has risen above it all. I Am writing this to help you understand what and where you need to begin to work to help your soul, your life, your being. And if you refuse to accept it, then that is simply your loss. I do not like it when you go against My word. And when you actually believe that I side with you against someone, and you do not have enough of Me to know that they are innocent, then you have not paid enough attention to My Word. Can you imagine what I think about someone who suffers under the abuse of people who dare puff themselves up to believe that they know what is in the heart of someone who is Mine? Imagine how serious it is to assume that you can dare withhold kindness from anyone. Think about how evil it is in My Presence that when you are kind for small moments you actually think you are doing them and Me a favor.

Every person around her, she strove to love. Her heart was poured out to children and that was evil spoken of. Those who were jealous of her love for those children would talk behind her back as though she was casting spells when all she ever did was obey Me in love, real sincere love. The day she had to give up those children, it put her flat on her back. An illness that she had for two years surfaced because her grief of loss of all she loved affected her immune system. And I was the only One who cared, the only One who knew the truth.

People took her name and used it to prove that they have God. They took what seemed to be the truth to them, and they used that name which was and is precious in My sight and told untrue testimonies to make themselves look as though they are what they claim. And these people to this day do not have the power to change their lives. Until you make it right before Me, you can never be released from the hold of My Word. As I said before, silence and patience would have worked better than to claim that you are something that you are not. She had Jesus, and He took over for her. Where she could not bear it, He did. Where she could not defend herself, He did and does.

Focusing on Me, she had little or no understanding for the Word; therefore, she knew nothing about how to defend herself, and mix it with her mental inability, there is no way without My grace that she would have lived through one day. For years of her newborn Christian life, she had gone through so many things, things that many of you have yet to go through. Nothing I have said, nothing that you could imagine, nothing could ever give you a real picture of what it was like for her. And no matter what I tell you, it is only the tip of the iceberg. At the end of those trial years, I covered her with My wings. She was always covered, but it was then that I made it real to her. She could see My wings and feel them and feel them shut out the whole world and felt the awesome protection that they bring. Even though she was under My protection, I had never revealed her purpose until a month ago. For thirty years she was attacked repeatedly from every direction: mentally, emotionally, and physically. She was being bombarded so continually, so hard that she almost died many, many times. Try to picture it in your own mind what it would be like to walk into a room and know and feel exactly what was being spoken about you that was so devastatingly evil and detestable and dead wrong and never defend yourself, never speak out against it, and never hold one thing in your heart against anyone for their ignorance and lack of understanding. Try to understand she had no capacity within her to fight even in the Spirit. You had a sound mind and many abilities, and because you made her appear evil with your tongue, you thought that I was with you. Think again. She had no idea or understanding to pray the way you did. She had to learn how to defend herself by living and breathing in Me. Oh, I hope you get this. I hope you understand what I am saying to you. I will explain just a little bit further. Some things never disappear out of your life by rebuking it, by rebuking the enemy, by saying magic words that wave a wand. It will always come back because it is not put down through the presence and the power of the Word living and breathing in you through the very first principles of taking Jesus so completely into your heart that *He endures for you.* I know some of you don't understand that, but I pray that you do, because this truly is Jesus Christ. This is the way He lived; this is the way He endured, He thought, and He felt when these things were done to Him. And now they are being done to My children. There is a way out, you know. Bring it to Me, dear children, but when you do remember to permit Me to work it out with you in detail that the enemy of your soul can never bring it back to you again. Remember also to make it right, to speak to the person that you hurt this way and tell them how not only wrong you were but how sorry you are for what you did. Pride will try to keep you from it. Some of you went on a little journey and sought out perhaps one thing and said, "I'm done; I got it all right now." You have no idea of what degree the Word holds you when you have had the audacity to hold even one person to it.

I taught her that if after many years a memory of pain comes to you about a past offense, it is only because it hasn't been truly forgiven. Because once you are offended by someone, if you do not tell Me these words, "I forgive them, Lord," you will never be forgiven. The memory of the offense gets erased out of your mind once you truly forgive. Especially when you pray with a full knowledge that it is being erased out of your memory the way your sins are erased out of Mine. If I come to you and give it to you as a testimony to help another, it is never coming from you, but you had better be sure that it is from Me. Many of you are saying things to millions of people right now that are not from Me, and you claim they are.

When a person comes into the church and you think they are naked and you see everything, remember it is you who are naked to Me. When your discernment spreads evil lies about people, it is not discernment. If I reveal something to you, I would never dishonor anyone by spreading it around. A humble heart knows this. You need to repent, and when you let it slide for years and do nothing to make it right, you only rob yourself. Luke 12:13, 14 (KJV) says, "And one of the company said unto Him, Master, speak to my brother, that he divide the inheritance with me. And He said unto him, *Man, who made me a judge or a divider over you?*" Now if Jesus did not choose between two brothers and if He did not commit Himself to any one particular man knowing what was in all men, then why would I be with you in telling others anything about anybody, and why would I be with you in any disagreement, any misunderstanding, any argument, or any fight? I teach plainly to leave others alone. How much plainer can I get than to tell you that if they are following Me, if they know that My Son is the Son of God, if they worship in the name of Jesus as they ought to leave them alone, I Am able to save Mine to the uttermost?

I Am not speaking to those preachers and teachers that have taught almost every aspect of the gospel in the uttermost detail. They didn't preach and teach their church doctrine. They didn't preach and teach their church history. They taught you plainly the things that I revealed to many of them personally. Now, during this time in the church, it is going to be a time of growing up. Where you once depended on others to do your homework, you are going to be left behind. Right now you have to work on catching up. Those you saw who really served Me and you chose to not go. You chose to say that it was for them and not you made a terrible mistake because all of you are called to have as close a walk with Me as possible. For you it is safe.

The vessel that is writing this book was called to a very special task. She has a special anointing that enabled her to overcome and endure all alone, just her and Me. Some of you are tempted to believe that if a person goes through great persecution or misunderstanding or oppression, surely they did something wrong and that they should not tell others about it. If this vessel doesn't tell it, then she cannot fulfill her calling. Some of you believe that you should let go of your past and your failures, and truly they are to be let go of, by the flesh. But never let go of your victories. This vessel in Me has *millions* of victories to share in order to help others get through their little ones. I Am determined to reveal Myself in her life to ensure that any puffed-up judge, any puffed-up prophet, any puffed-up preacher, or any puffed-up teacher could clearly hear that I will visit their sin. And if you say you have no sin, you will be found to be a liar. For once I name it, I assure you it is there. The kind of persecution that she endured for years was only achieved in victory because Jesus Christ lived within her through the Word. It was the anointing that He walked and talked on the earth. She read the Word over and over in order to have Him take over when she needed Him to.

Isn't it any wonder that all of her life, every day, every moment, every penny, every thought, every atom of her being belonged to Me, that when she needed to be healed without asking Me I would be there to heal her? When she was so ill that she completely lost her memory to such a degree that she could not read her own name, inside of her was already planted My Word, not by memorization, not by repetition, but by belief. She read the scripture that said that the Holy Spirit brings all things to your remembrance. When she first became ill and had such bad times with her memory, and when it began to fade, she would look up and say, "Lord, Your Word promised me that you would bring all things to my remembrance." And she would just rest and wait, and what she needed to remember would come to her just like I promised. And when she had not the capacity to think, to form any thoughts, or to pray, I was able to call her by name; and she would through My Spirit instantly realize it was her name. She would be driving in a car and suddenly forget where she was going, who she was, and what anything was. Imagine driving and not knowing what a car was. And I would speak to her and tell her who was the person sitting next to her and tell her to go to the right and then turn to the left, and she was going to go to their house. In 1999, this was her condition that was slowly getting worse. All the while she endured this memory loss, she never panicked or became afraid because she held My hand securely. And when they said her physical condition was so bad that surely she must be enduring panic attacks, they sent her to a therapist. And that therapist could clearly see that she needed no help and told her that all of the books in her office were written for people in her condition and how the therapist could clearly see she did not need any help. So she asked her, "How did you get this way?" And her answer was "I read my Bible." No truer words were ever spoken. That therapist began to cry and pour out her heart to her, and she ministered to the one who was supposed to help her.

You would have to imagine what it would be like to have an ongoing illness with a memory condition and wind up lying in a bed for almost a year. She was wrapped up in an electric blanket turned up on the high setting. She had her head wrapped, her hands with several pairs of gloves, with several pairs of socks; and her teeth chattered because she was so cold. The fibromyalgia caused such an exaggeration of pain that her sinuses gave her headaches that would cause her to scream. She had spasms in her bladder and in her bowels that caused her to scream with pain. Every bone in her body hurt so much that if she touched a sheet, she would scream in agony. She had an ovarian tumor growing with a mass within her, wrapping itself around her organs. She was unable to take one step without the stress to her heart beating so hard that she breathed as though she had run fifty miles an hour. One step, just one step was agonizing pain. Her legs felt like two five-hundred-pound weights that she could not lift, and she strove so hard to move just one tiny step. She had times of absolute oblivion where one day ran into the next with no sense of time, no sense of anything except agony. She threw up every single day, and her body would just freeze up on her where she could not function to think at all. She had lost all use of her right arm, it was like a hanging rag. She could not walk anymore. No one came to pray for her, and if anyone did come, they visited her as though they were doing her such a favor just showing up. They were all talking at the church that surely she had to have sinned and that she was going to die. And so when they came, she told them that she was not going to die, but live. I am telling you that if you think she suffered this because she had sinned so much more than you, you need to repent.

She had a television set directly in front of her that her husband had set up for her, which played tapes day and night of John Hagee preaching. At times she couldn't understand them, she couldn't really hear them; and because she is extremely nearsighted, she could not see them. But she was grateful that the Word was being preached. And suddenly I opened up her eyes, and she saw and felt Jesus lean over and whisper in her ear. Ever so gently, ever so softly, and He said, "Merienne, do you believe that I love you?" And instantly she responded, lifting up to get closer, "Yea, Lord, I believe." And she then saw Jesus lean over her and shove His face into Satan's who was leaning over her on the other side, and Jesus said very strongly, "See! I told you she would believe!" And she got up, and I stood before her. She began to pray with all her heart for those whom she loved that had hurt her so much. And she did this with a sincere, unpretended love. To her once again, as I stood suddenly before her, I was huge; she could not see My face. But she knew she did not need to. My Presence was so powerful before her; and it was more than when I touched her and healed her of cancer, more than when I healed her husband, through her, of alcoholism. She could see this tremendous light, the white robe, and all My Glory as I laid My hand on her head and spoke over her the way any preacher would speak over you at the altar. And she was instantly healed of this devastating disease that sought to kill her. After a period of time and it was hours, not days, she still had the fibromyalgia; and she told Me that if this was her quality of life, she wanted to die. And I said, "You cannot handle this alone. Call the John Hagee ministry." And she did. Someone in his ministry prayed over the telephone for her, and within ten minutes, she was completely healed.

So many people are held in bondage to the prognosis of the doctor. He goes by the symptoms he sees. The voice of the disease or problem the enemy is trying to get you to receive to yourself and sometimes those symptoms are nothing but lies. From the moment the symptoms begin to speak, you need to resist the power of them over your body. Satan's power was broken over you at the moment of conversion. The only power he has left is to deceive you. And he can only do that if you let him. And the only way you would let him is if you do not fill up your mind and heart with Jesus by filling yourself up with the Word. My people perish because of their lack of knowledge of Me. Hosea 4:6

(KJV) says, "My people are destroyed for lack of knowledge: because thou hast rejected knowledge, I will also reject thee, that thou shalt be no priest to me: seeing thou hast forgotten the law of thy God, I will also forget thy children." You may go to an altar of prayer. You can feel and bask in My Presence and all your symptoms disappear and then you go home and they seem to all return and you believe the lie that I did not touch you *when I did. You deny My Presence* which you felt so much when you went for prayer, and then when the enemy attacks you, you say that I did not heal you. Therefore, you wind up seemingly in the same condition, and you blame everybody but yourself. It has to be the preacher's fault that laid hands on you. Being foolish, you may even discuss it with friends and begin to discuss with your mouth what you believe in your heart, that you didn't get healed. When had you been filled with the Word the way this vessel was? The temptation to receive the symptom would come, but because *abiding* within her was the Word which is Jesus, *He* was able to raise her up with the Presence of My Spirit and put the enemy, the symptom, to flight. You lose out because the Word which is Jesus Christ cannot rise up within you and resist the temptations to receive the symptoms once again. But no, no one wants to spend time in the Word. It is no profit to the flesh. And the flesh lusts after entertainment, it lusts after feeling good and instant satisfaction. Your flesh doesn't want to endure, and it lies to your mind that you just don't have to work or labor like that. Well, then you don't get what you need.

This vessel came to me about every disease that attacked her and asked me this, "What if I don't have access to anyone else to pray for me? And what if I am on medication and something terrible happens and I am not able to have it? How am I going to continue to believe if I depend on medication to help me? What if I don't have the money to go to the doctors or get medication?" Her prayer was for Me to help her to overcome *everything* that she will not have to take any medication or depend on any other person other than Me. She simply refused to give anyone or anything the power over her life. She said, "If I die, I die, but I'm not giving the enemy the glory. I will die with God in my heart and in my mind." And I Am still within her heart and within her mind.

99

When she was so ill that she couldn't walk or function as I have described, by 2005 she had a heart attack because of the damage to her heart. (Lupus does damage to your organs.) That heart attack weakened her heart considerably. She was told by doctors that she had to have had blocked arteries. This was in a different state, and they did not have her medical history. She told them how she was healed of cancer, lupus, fibromyalgia, osteoporosis, an ovarian tumor and mass; and the heart doctor sat down and put both of his hands on the sides of his face with his head down and rocked from side to side as though to say to himself, "Oh no, not another one of these nuts." He lifts his head and says, "Look, we know you had a heart attack, and we know it had to have come about because of blocked arteries, and now we are going to prove it." So they sent her down for a test that puts dye in her arteries, and she was awake just enough to see them gasp as they saw that her arteries were completely clear. She confessed with her mouth what she believed in her heart, and I was able to save her. Listen to what I say. Her confession wasn't a forced confession of repeating words that held no meaning for her. Her confession wasn't something she was trying to believe. She *had the Word abiding within her that what she believed in her heart had substance for her faith.* What did she believe in her heart? She believed exactly what she read in the Word about Jesus. She did not walk around confessing over and over her faith to make it work like magic words. She had put the Word there, and the Word rose up and did the fighting for her. In every single occasion, the *Word did the work, through the presence of the Holy Spirit,* with *both abiding within her.*

When they said they wanted to put her on high blood pressure medication because it was slightly elevated, she commanded her blood pressure to obey the Holy Spirit within her, and she saw it on the blood pressure cup go down to 120 over 80. Now at the doctor's office it is always 120 over 80, and in a few days she will be sixty-five years old. They tried every heart medication there was to settle down her heartbeat. Some of the medicines worked the opposite, and the heartbeat stopped dead and took way too long between beats. They tried everything that they knew how to do, to get her heart into rhythm. They would get her ready for the electric paddles, and just before they used them on her,

her heart would kick into rhythm of 72. They would take her back to her room; it would kick out and be 157 or 190. Everybody would look at the computer monitor and watch her heart go way out of course, so wild they described it, as it must have felt like it was going to break out of her chest. She told them more like her chest and then her back. They all feared so much for her life that when it was in this condition, they would slowly creep into the room to see what she was doing; they thought perhaps she was not resting. They were fearful that if she did not know her heart was acting up and if they told her that, she would react like so many do in fear and make it worse. They crept quietly only to find her sitting on the edge of the bed, and she was praying for someone who was dying of cancer. Then they asked her, "Don't you feel that?" And she said, "Of course I do, it's my heart." But *my Bible says that men's heart fails them through fear, and I am not afraid. So my heart will not quit ticking.* Finally they did an ablation, and it still was out of rhythm for four months. They told her that she had a leaking valve that caused the other valve to overwork itself and it was swollen and caused the irregular heartbeats. Had she listened to the doctor, had she listened to her heart, she would be dead. But she listened to Me. She commanded her heart to obey the Holy Spirit within her in the name of Jesus Christ, and it went into rhythm so perfectly that the heart doctor took her off of all her medication.

When a doctor tells her something, she never believes it if I didn't tell her. She doesn't go to the doctor's waiting room, waiting for them to give her any answers. She waits on Me to tell her. She believes Me. When she was in such excruciating pain that it would cause her to want to die, she did as I instructed her. She resisted it and commanded it to go. Eventually it did. Now it disappears in a moment. She learned not to give in to it. She learned not to pay any attention to the symptom. She learned to pay attention to Me. And now she is free and healthier than ever before at the age of sixty-five. They said that her heart was weak and damaged so much that she wouldn't be able to do the things that she used to do. Right now she is able to do all the things that the doctors said she would never be able to do again. She didn't stop taking her medication; she waited until I revealed to the doctor that she didn't need it. She sought Me first, and if I told her that she was fine, she resisted to the death, and several times she almost did die. But she won the victory and brought glory to My Name. Because now the doctors write on her chart the word "healed," not "cured," but "healed." Is this what you do? All these details can teach you so much about how to obey Me when dying. It would do you good to read them.

Every time she would get close to death, she would ask Me, "Is it my time to meet You, Lord?" And I would bring to her remembrance the things that I had promised to use her for. In doing this, it was like when Paul wasn't concerned about a shipwreck killing him because God had told him that he would get to Rome, and then he knew that he would be delivered out of the shipwreck. He knew that the snake could not kill him. She now preaches and teaches that unless God personally comes to you and tells you that it is time to go home, you need to fight and resist the devil's power to take your life to the last breath. For sometimes it will be victorious in the last breath.

These things are written to give you enough understanding as to why very few people truly receive a healing even though the person they go to for prayer is tremendously anointed. It goes to a place that is the same with everything else according to how much you obey My Word. The people who have ministries for healing are very faithful; they have done their part, and you are the one who needs to do your part. I Am not saying that every person who claims that God is with them to heal has Him there to do the operation; what I Am telling you is that I have men and women who are used by Me to heal.

She has learned as a Christian to throw the devil's words right back at him. If the enemy tells her that she doesn't feel good, she will say that is the one thing that will not happen. She will feel good because God promised her that victory. Every word that he tempts her with, she throws right in his face. Now some of you will take this and use it *without* Me and as usual apply the principle without Me, and for a while it will seem to work, but when you truly expect it and need it, I simply won't be there. The time will come where nothing will seem to work until you do what your preachers have been preaching for years. *Get into My Word and pray.* Only for some of you, you may be left behind.

So far behind that it may become impossible to catch up when I come and shut the door. Today is the day of salvation. Today is the day to heed the call. Even believing that the Word has a magic formula just by repeating it will seem to be enough. The truth is that the Word has to be ingested as part of your being within your heart and your mind. A daily devotional on someone else's experience and understanding or revelation will not help you half as much as getting a Word from Me. There is nothing wrong with a daily devotional, but there is something wrong when you use it as your only source of contact with Me because you want to enjoy yourself and be entertained or entertain the flesh the rest of the time. There is nothing wrong with self-help books written by Holy Spirit-inspired authors. But there is something wrong with them being your only source of reading the Word of God for yourself. No one, no matter who you are, can continually grow on the revelation of another. You need a certain amount of it yourself. And you can only obtain it in the Word alone, just you and Me. Many preachers preach what they have learned from other preachers. This vessel gets all of her revelation of truth directly from Me.

There is also nothing wrong with television evangelists. But they were never intended to be your *only* source of church service. You are robbing yourself of the truth. You will not be in heaven all alone. It is impossible for a television preacher to know you the way a local pastor will. It is impossible to interact with the children of God in church by watching a television service. For the personal fellowship that I intended among you is lacking in watching a service. Interacting with people who are Mine does something that watching cannot do. It helps you grow in a way that you cannot grow any other way. People who have no Holy Spirit-filled churches in their area and people who are unable to attend church service for whatever reason need these preachers. I sent these preachers, and they need to be able to reach as many people as possible. Their works in the mission field is something that all of you cannot do. It is the only source for shut-ins. All that you do with any ministry that you cannot physically attend, even the books you read, should be in accordance to going to your local church, in accordance with *you* reading the Bible for yourself. If you have no Holy Spirit-filled church in your area, then get yourself in the position to go and be used by Me, to be used as an example of what a true believer is in worship, reading your Bible, rightly dividing the Word of truth; and I promise you the people around you will change as you lift Me up. I will draw all men unto Me. I did not say you go in and take over. I did not say for you to go into any church and think that you are going to bind and rebuke and control any church. Anything that you do that manipulates will be made manifest to all. You go humbly seeking to help rather than be helped, you go humbly seeking to understand rather than be understood, you go humbly seeking to lift others rather than be lifted, you go humbly seeking to love rather than be loved, and you cannot fail with that attitude.

Don't twist any of these words up to say that I Am not with these television preachers because I Am. Don't think I am saying do not listen to them because without them you would have *no* revelation. You have been too lazy to seek it, so they did it for you. What I Am saying is that you need them all. You need to continue with your self-help books, continue with those you believe you were called to watch their service, but do not use them as your excuse to not go into the Word by yourself or go to your local church or come to Me by yourself. I did call every person that watches them. They are tremendous men and women of God, and I love them and I sent them, and I will not have any twist up My words and make them into something that I Am not intending or saying. If you have been offended, then take a good look at yourself as to why you are not filled with Christ enough to *love beyond* that *offense.*

The devil kept telling her that she is getting older, and she can't do these things. I kept telling her that she is stronger, and she can do everything. For a while after she was healed, because she lay in bed so long it weakened her muscles, and she had to grip a banister to pull herself upstairs. She had to go through physical therapy to be able to walk again. She knew that her ability to walk was so much better than struggling just to lift one leg up one-eighth of an inch like she used to do, before she was healed. Being able to overcome cancer in the last stages with excruciating pain and extreme weakness is a victory in Christ. Her spirit at times slipped out of her body. She knew what death felt like. And when you defeat the taking of your mind whether it is in the memory or in the emotions of being mentally ill without medication or a doctor, that is a victory in Christ. I do not expect you to be like her, but I do expect you to understand and realize that if I did it for her, I can and will do it for you. I love her no more or no less than I do you. Although I completely love and enjoy My fellowship with her.

None of these things came to pass within her in a moment, and this is the answer most people are looking for. They come to Me, and I give it right back to them to work it all out with Me, and many of them don't hear. Somewhere along the line, there is a great misunderstanding about what I do and what I will or will not do. Your miracles are within your faith, within your grasp, within your doings, within you. And when you do not receive it from someone else, then you need to realize I have not given you what you have been seeking the way you seem to believe that I want you to seek it. Her lupus lifted in a moment, but the physical therapy and the memory had to be dealt with slowly, and it all came back to her. Because as her faith was, so was it done unto her. This is why I say that her healings are enough to write a lot of books on, and they will have the missing link between God and man in reception of healing and why.

No matter what is written here, there is no way that you could ever imagine what it was like for her to live through one day for years. Because of her mental and emotional problems at first it was the agony of living a life without knowing Me. And the mental, emotional agony of getting through one day was unbelievable. And it was almost unendurable to face day after day, month after month, year after year; and it became more than she could handle. Before she met Me, she was very suicidal. And as a Christian, she patiently waited upon Me. Believing with all her heart that what she desired would come to pass. And do you want to know what she desired? At first all she wanted was to be normal, to be able to live life, and to face anything with a sound mind. She could see the gap between where she was mentally and where she needed to be. She had no ability to communicate with others. (Look at her now.) Then as a Christian, that desire changed into wanting to be able to reach out and help someone in her condition. To make sure that she would never dishonor or hurt My cause. All of her thinking and feelings, no matter where the condition came from, the *desire she has is to do My will*. That desire came from her putting the Word in her until Jesus was able to thrive and live within her with the desire to do My will. You put Him in you to defeat the enemy for something you want. You put Him in you to obtain whatever your need is. You put Him within you for an immediate release of whatever the oppression is. But because Christ lives within a vessel like this one, they will put Him inside of them to do My will. Take a good look at what you are reading and strive to comprehend that she would never have been able to endure all or any of this had she not had the "abiding Word" within her.

How you see yourself is very important. I agree with this kind of teaching. But to take your image and make it something that it isn't or try to obtain some easier way or some other spoken magic formula words is wrong. You must see yourself with Jesus Christ living within you, not as dead words, proving that you have no true relationship with God. Not envisioning it and calling it meditation. Put Him in you as dead words and He might as well be still on your shelf. Apply it daily. Apply it in everything in everyday living; then you will have something that cannot be robbed, cannot be stolen, nor cannot be forgotten. Once the Word lives and breathes in you through a reality of a relationship between you and Me, then you have something that will endure through everything throughout all eternity.

You have heard the scripture of the five wise and five foolish virgins. Some of you imagine that surely this means that the five foolish did not take the anointing of the Holy Spirit with them. Their lamps were not trimmed with God's presence. Well, to a point that truth is true. But I Am saying that if you don't have the anointing that comes *only through the Word living within you*, it is impossible to trim your lamp without it. One part of Me is not enough; you must have all three abiding. Whatever you build upon, whatever you base your faith on determines whether you stand or fall. There comes a day in every man's life that I will visit, and when I do, all that is not the way I have intended it to be for My will to be done will fall. It will look so close, it will seem so right. Because all the teaching of the Holy Spirit that has been done up until now is perfect except for one thing. You cannot and will not have the fullness of the anointing without the Word of God. Some of you know this. You have done this; but many of you take what is being taught, what I have sent for you to hear, and put it in the wrong place, or you take a small part and apply it where you have wants and needs. Because of the flesh being in control instead of the Spirit, you might as well have put Me back on a shelf. You render Me useless in your life. What makes you believe that I will tolerate a soul continually doing this? I love you too much to permit you to deceive yourself so much that you can't in the end get in. You will now have to work in "catching up." And if you don't, you will be left behind. The hour is too short to play with the things of Me the way you have been playing for years. You will remember that I warned you.

If you take heed to the things I am telling you even now. Just as she was all alone and persecuted, she was so hated in most cases without cause, so criticized day and night about everything. That the pressure would be so great in the human that she would suddenly not want to live and take the vehicle she was driving and try to commit suicide with it. I would be there, and as she turned the car into the direction of destruction, *I* turned the wheel of the car in the opposite direction. She could feel Me take over. She knew that it was Me, but she was determined to kill herself. And she fought against Me until she became so exhausted from fighting that she parked the car and listened to Me tell her to go on. That there was a day that was coming that I would bless her and how she would rejoice. Now why do you think that I would care that a woman like her would be so much under pressure in every direction that I would save her life? What makes you think that with that kind of mental pressure it would not drive you so crazy that suddenly you would decide to end it all? Would I be there for you under such circumstances? I will tell you that if you served Me, as she did, I would. If you loved Jesus the way she did, I would. I also intervened to *prove* through this testimony that *I can, I will, and I do intervene against your fleshy will.*

As you can plainly see, I overrode her free will. Her desire and will at that moment was to die. It is not true that I will not override your free will, because the moment that you give your life to Me, *you gave me complete power to override everything in your life.* You cannot come to a king and submit to Him with your vow to a covenant and expect that king to be such a gentle person that He would never deal with you. I am *not* telling you that if you try to commit suicide I will be there to override your desire. Don't be so foolish. I knew her heart. I understood how to help her. Many kill themselves without my intervention because I know their hearts. This testimony is to reveal to you a truth that once you give Me your life, you are giving Me permission to intervene when I need to. Whether I have to deal with you harshly or gently, *I will deal.* Isn't it better to make sure that I do not have to deal with you harshly?

My church has preached for a long, long time, pleading with you for a long, long time for you to repent and turn away from your wicked ways and I will heal your land. The message from those who are Mine has always been to get into the Word and pray. There are those that are so foolish they keep applying it to others and never see that I have not healed their land, so what is wrong? Oh, that you would have listened.

Ask yourself, could you endure being sworn at and lied on by everybody in your life, not just one or two but everyone, and still be able to walk among all of them filled with the love of Christ so much that the Holy Spirit would be able to convict souls enough to see them saved and led to repentance? As Paul the Apostle said, they will have their reward. It doesn't matter how they saw it, and it doesn't matter what they thought. When I touched this vessel, I justified her, and I protect and keep her even now. Those false accusers need to realize, are they safe in the arms of Christ now? When they pray, do they always walk, talk, and feel My presence with them; or has all their doings come upon their heads enough that they still suffer trouble? You endure one small problem concerning even your own children, and you are ready to destroy, and yet you think that I would give you the power to pick apart what I tell her. You have so much to learn. And the way to learn it is not by depending on the gift that I have given you to save others. I Am not speaking of the gift of the Holy Spirit, I Am speaking of the gift of prophecy, the gift of healing, and the gift of faith; because although these are gifts of the Holy Spirit, *I never intended for you to depend upon them to save you.* Some of you sit back and rest in the fact that I use you, and you never realize that you need to rest in the fact *that Jesus saved you.*

I sent her to a church years ago, and when I did, I told her that I wanted her to go there. She had attended it several times and decided that she liked traveling farther away because the church she enjoyed more was there. This church was little, and she liked it but did not want to attend it. Both of these churches taught babies in their messages, and there was nowhere in the area that she lived to receive meat. She had Me though. I told her to go there, and she flatly refused, all the while she was showering to go. She said again no, all the while she went to the car, and she was driving to the church. I said, "I need you to deliver a message in this church, and when you go, you will know why." She marveled at how I would override her will as she found herself in the church. *My word within her was full, so much so that I could lead her in spite of herself. For the self in her was all too weak to resist Me. Listen to what I Am saying, the self within her was too weak to resist My will. She had died to herself.* She sat down as the preacher began to cry about how someone was persecuting poor him. Mind you, he suffered only one person's persecution, and he had all of his elders and preacher friends there supporting him and holding his hand all the while he cried.

I led her to stand and testify how much persecution and lies she had to endure all the while she had been told she was dying of cancer. I will not write it all in this book, but it amounted to a terrible persecution from everyone including her family and neighbors. Many people cursed and swore at her without knowing her or even meeting her, and many spread lies on her, and it was without cause. I say this because no one deserves to be lied upon, cursed, or any such thing. And many persecuted her child and spread evil lies on her, and in spite of that she would dare not forgive any of them. And when she began to testify of My Glory and how I delivered her and how she said not a word to anyone, all of the leaders in this church went to the altar. And some of you who call yourselves prophets do not realize that you go through so little and endure so little that you have no idea what I have spared you from. And you have earned no right to judge what she says. Remember, it is I that uses your mouth, and that ability to speak was never given to defend and protect you. Not one prophecy will I ever send because you did not like what another had said about you. For prophecy is not for your personal use. And since it isn't, then why do you dare get so offended. You get so offended that you have a hard time forgiving. As I have lifted you up, remember that you are not in control and will never tell Me what to do about anything. For I do not hear because you think you are hurt. I hear because I have My own desire and purpose to lift up My Son and glorify Him and not you.

If this vessel lifted herself up at any time, I assure you that I would not have written any of these words. But because she never used Me as some of you have, I Am able to fulfill My Word within her. I defend My Word that I put within her heart, within her mind, and within her mouth. Will I do the same for you? She has the power to discern what is you and what is Me, and although she will never mention your name to anyone, she will never mention your name to Me in a bad light. I will mention your name to her in any light I so choose because I trust her. Do I say the same about you?

Years ago I called her again to go to another church other than the one she loved. Many of you think when I tell you this that I Am calling you to another church when all I Am asking is for you to visit. She did the same thing as she did the last time I called her. She told me flatly no. All the while she got up and got dressed, totally forgetting that We had been through this before. I told her that I had someone who was coming from thousands of miles away to give her a gift. She fought Me all the way. She continually argued with Me. This is something that unless you are as yielded to Me through My Spirit and My Word, I suggest you never try this. She had suffered and endured so much that she had not yet been healed from much of it, and that is why I let so much go. Her mercy for others, her compassion for all others was so great that I Am true to My Word, and I Am merciful and compassionate with her *always*. She found herself getting out of the car to go into the church and still insisted that she wasn't going in. As she sat down, someone from behind the pulpit that she had never seen before opened up his mouth and said, "I have come from thousands of miles away today to give someone a gift from God." Her mouth dropped open. This man was a prophet from Africa; she could plainly feel the powerful Presence of My Spirit. And she went to the altar, and as she stood there, she could feel the awesome anointing of My Spirit that cast out any and all demons in people as he walked by. When he came into her presence, he put his hand on her head and paused for a moment. Then he said, "Give her what she needs, Lord." She fell under the power of My Spirit but rose up very disappointed. Because when he spoke, her mind said, "This is my gift? That's all it is, a blessing?" She had no idea that I never bless with My Presence without doing something for you. At that time, My presence was being taken so lightly by her, with no understanding.

So disappointed, she walked to the car and tried to turn the key, and I told her to go back, and she refused. But she could not turn the key, and her body went right back. And I told her to tell him exactly why she was sent to the church. She went up to him and told him, and he said, "Well, let's pray about it and e-mail each other or call on the telephone when I get back to Africa." She thanked him and turned around to walk away, and he said, "Wait, let me pray for you." When he laid his hand on her head, she will to this day never forget it. She felt the awesome power of Living Waters flowing through every part of her physical brain, and she opened up her mouth and began to speak in tongues. And when she woke up out of the Spirit, she said to him, "*That was the gift*," and he praised the Lord with her. She did call him, and he fasted and prayed for her for five days. And her life was truly blessed through this tremendous African man who is the greatest prophet she has ever known.

Amazing, isn't it? She has personally received letters from those whom she considers the greatest prophets of our time. The respect she has is awesome because she knows who are Mine. And I promised her that any prophet who is Mine will recognize Me in her, and that is how she will know who is who. For those who are lifted up will never see how great I Am in her. They only see how great they think they are. And they will respond accordingly.

Is it any wonder that this person who wrote this book would have been filled so much with the anointing of Jesus Christ through the presence of the Holy Spirit that they could live through it all enough to see My Presence in a cloud in her room? She would see Me in the room often. See Me standing at her door when she was home alone. Feel My hand shake her shoulder and awaken her to pray to save someone's life in intercessory prayer. See Me tuck her into bed at night when someone cursed her. She needed that because for years, there was never any understanding, any comfort, any love from anyone. She was surrounded with people who worked their witchcraft of control against her, and every time they spun a lie, they now have that lie on their own soul. And they must now have to wonder why they are enduring and suffering. They need to repent. Psalm 18:4-6 (KJV) says, "The sorrows of death compassed me, the floods of ungodly men made me afraid. The sorrows of hell compassed me about: the snares of death prevented me. In my distress I called upon the LORD, and cried unto my God: He heard my voice out of His temple and my cry came before Him, even into his ears." This is something that I did when My Son died, when He gave His life up willingly. I came to earth personally, and the moment He died, there was a great earthquake, and many rose from their graves. This is something that is within the true Christian when they willingly give up their life that Jesus may live within. I deliver and have delivered and will deliver.

Is it any wonder that when she went to bed at night with no one to love her I would brush her forehead with a good-night kiss? I did not speak through another vessel and say or show them that I kissed her. I kissed her. And she felt the brush of it upon her forehead. And she felt the love with which it was given. Is it any wonder that when someone punched her in the mouth full force My hand was there, and she felt nothing? She felt only a feather touch her cheek. Is it any wonder that suddenly she could feel My Presence so strongly and within her she wondered why, and when she turned around she could see a person with an iron poker held above her head and trying with all their strength to bring it down upon her head and they could not. One, two, three attempts until the stress of trying to destroy her was so exhausting that all they could do was walk over to the fire and stoke it. The poker was cold, and yet it bent as the coals were stoked because the demon was that strong, but never as strong as I. Is it any wonder that when she fell and broke her hand bones into her wristbone I healed it instantly? She felt it break, she heard it crack, and she didn't cry out with pain, nor did she seek anyone else's help although I sent them to take her to the hospital emergency room. She simply looked at Me and said, "Where are Your angels, Lord? You promised they would bear me up." They put a temporary cast on her, and she tore it off that night because it hurt so badly with it on. And she marveled that it was so instantly healed. So the next day when she went to see the bone specialist and he came into the room, he told her she had really done some job on her wristbone, because he had seen the x-rays. He folded his fingers together to show how they crushed and splintered into each other. He was in such a hurry and quickly said how he saw the x-ray and then looked down and saw that she did not have a cast on her wrist. The shock of the healing caused him to shake, and he could hardly speak without stuttering. At that time she had a team of five doctors taking care of her with having lupus, and they all were told about her healing. Doctors got to a point that if she had a problem and she told them that she had prayer for it, they would say, "We are not going to touch it, not even to test it to see if it is true. For we will not touch what God has already done."

Today I have put this vessel safely in a local church. When she entered the door the first time, they invited her back. She told them, "To go to this church because you invited me is a poor reason to choose this church. To come to this church because a friend, neighbor, parent, or anybody invited me is a very poor reason to attend this church. But I ask you to pray for me. That I get into the church that God called me to go to. Because I know that if God chooses the church, everything will flow through the presence of the Holy Spirit." She decided to go to the church at least three times before making up her mind. And during that time, she saw the love that they had for souls, for God, and the work they labor to do in Christ. It was the Lord she had known for years and recognized Jesus in them. To her, these people were like taking a long cool drink of water. Not because she was able to tell them all the things that had happened to her because she did not. Not because she told one side of a story and found refuge; it was the sincere love there for every soul. This is Jesus Christ. These pastors are strong and powerful in the

Lord. They preach and teach the truth, and they can teach you how to pick up your cross daily and follow Jesus.

Take this to heart and understand what I am saying. Holy Spirit-filled men and women have preached for a very long time. "Get into the Word, read your Bible, and pray." This call has been across the world to My church for years. If you were to ask Me how many took heed, I would have to tell you very little. They only seem to be reborn; they only seem to be committed. They absolutely refuse to get into the Word and learn of Me. Many are still in darkness, for the light has not been able to cause them to come out of the womb. Not because the light is not powerful enough but because they refuse. Satan's power is not because he is so powerful, it is because many *give* him willingly that much power over them.

PART IX

"Then shall the kingdom of heaven be likened unto ten virgins, which took their lamps, and went forth to meet the bridegroom. And five of them were wise, and five were foolish. They that were foolish took their lamps and took no oil with them: But the wise took oil in their vessels with their lamps. While the bridegroom tarried, they all slumbered and slept. And at midnight there was a cry made, Behold the bridegroom cometh; go ye out to meet him. Then all those virgins arose, and trimmed their lamps. And the foolish said unto the wise, Give us of your oil; for our lamps are gone out. But the wise answered, saying Not so; lest there be not enough for us and you: but go ye rather to them that sell and buy for yourselves. And while they went to buy, the bridegroom came; and they that were ready went in with Him to the marriage: and the door was shut. Afterward came also the other virgins, saying, Lord, Lord, open to us. But He answered and said, Verily I say unto you, I know you not. Watch therefore, for ye know neither the day nor the hour wherein the Son of man cometh" (Matthew 25:1-13).

Understand they were virgins. They kept themselves untouched by the world, by the flesh, by the devil. They were virgins. Does that tell you something? It is not enough to resist Satan, it is not

115

enough to resist the world, it is not enough to resist the flesh. You must have the anointing of the Holy Spirit through the abiding Word Jesus Christ. Can you grasp hold of this?

Picture this in your mind and consider what I am saying. Matthew 25:1 (KJV) says, "Then shall the kingdom of heaven be likened unto ten virgins, which took their lamps, and went forth to meet the bridegroom."

Before we read any further, listen to how it has been taught. The oil to trim their lamps has always been taught as the Holy Spirit only. People in church welcome the Holy Spirit *which is My will.* They bask before Me, some dance, some sing, some speak in tongues, some interpret, and many go home not having the oil, the anointing of the Holy Spirit that can only come through Jesus Christ in the Word. *The Word is anointed, when He enters into you, you have His anointing.* Many experience only a small touch of Him at conversion and *never get into the Word to follow up.* He has to be a living, breathing experience to the fullest extent of the Word. I intended for the anointing of My Holy Spirit and the anointing of the Word which is My Son Jesus to operate *together.* Not in memorization. Although it is good to memorize, this is different. *The Word should become a part of you by experiencing Him in your life every day in everything,* and you need to ask yourself how He can do this if you never pick up the Word to read it. True discipleship comes within the church with those who are not necessarily preaching or teaching aspects of the Lord. It comes by helping souls learn what their Savior desires within them, by helping them to understand to continue in the Word *daily.*

You have a daily devotional and are satisfied that you can feel My Presence when you come to Me, and that little piece of Me and of the Word is enough for you. Nothing can turn out worse for you than for you to deliberately refuse to grow in grace, that you may grow the fruits that are so desperately needed within your Christian life. No, it is not true that anyone else is called to go into the word and study it to show them approved according to My Word and you not be called to it. Yes, there are seasons in your life and times that I will give you a little rest. But if you continue to believe that the little bit that you get daily is all I intended for you, you are very mistaken. Because *I called everyone to get into the word*, to study it that I may use *all.* For all of you have talents that I can use, and that is why they are given to you. And if you believe that you are to be having fun today while the world around you dies because you do not desire to learn enough to be able to even pray, you are very mistaken and need to repent. The enemy of your souls knows more than you do that this goes directly against the word as you claim the word, and he attacks you tremendously because your heart is not right with Me. Remember what I said in My word. Read Matthew 25:14-46. Read in particular Matthew 25:28, 29 (KJV), which says, "Take therefore the talent from him, and give it unto him which hath ten talents. For unto everyone that hath shall be given, and he shall have abundance: but from him that hath not shall be taken away even that which he hath." It has been said many times, what you think you have can disappear. All of you have talents that in Me will be developed and used, and when you refuse to work with Me to use them and believe that you are so special that I will not require you to labor as every Christian is to labor, you will need to answer to Me. Look around you. Are you blaming all others for your plight? Are you able to find true and real peace when you are bringing so much upon yourself? The positive and the negative of the Word are always in every life in operation. I promised that not one job or title will be changed and that all will be fulfilled. Rethink and consider the things that are written here. Take them to Me and I will help you. My desire is for your good. The enemy has it planned to lull you to sleep, and in the end get you discouraged and hurt you. My desire is to encourage you and lift you, and I can only do that through the Word, the way it was and is written.

I intended the Word to be the way it is written in John 17:3 (KJV), "And this is life eternal, that they might know Thee the only true God, and Jesus Christ, whom Thou hast sent." Now how can you know Jesus without making Him a part of your life through the Word? How? Okay, so you say, "Well, I hear preaching when I go to church." Some of you hear a little scripture read as though it is so far away from you and only something not attainable or only attainable for Jesus Christ and not for you. You may hear it one day a week. When you get up in the morning daily, you take a devotional and seem to be able to apply it to your day.

There is nothing wrong with that. But it is not enough. You borderline being like those who daily read their horoscopes. You use the Word the way you used to use the things of the devil. And because you claim the Word, you seem to be approved. But not by Me.

When you are tested and tried, you will have a difficult time enduring and hanging on to the little bit that you do know and understand. And still you never truly seek Jesus, the Word, or search out what you need to know. Jesus is still on the shelf, not doing you one bit of good. So many of you call your friends, your neighbors, your loved ones, telling them that you just need someone to talk to. Well, if that is the only comfort you seek, then you have it. But if you got on your knees in your heart and called on Me, what a friend you would have. I would and could do something about what you are going through.

PART X

"That they all may be one; as *Thou, Father, art in Me, and I in Thee, that they also may be one in Us*: that the world may believe that Thou hast sent Me. *I in them, and Thou in Me, that they may be made perfect in one; and that the world may know that Thou hast sent Me, and hast loved them, as Thou hast loved Me*" (John 17:21, 23 KJV).

I intended for the Word and the Holy Spirit to operate within you as one. You have no idea that you cannot operate in My fullness with just one. How can I abide within you if you render Me powerless in your life through neglecting the Word daily? I must tell you that I told you the world would cause you to have tribulation and that I would give you peace because I overcome the world. Knowing this doesn't happen unless you get the Word in you. And you are to pray for God to cause the Word to be a living, breathing part of you as you read and learn of Him. And My promise with everything else is that you will suffer persecution. You will have to endure. And trying to use Me to escape what I intended to glorify Myself in you with is not what I Am talking about. Matthew 16:21-23 (KJV) says, "Began Jesus to shew unto His disciples, how that He must go unto Jerusalem, and suffer many things of the elders and chief priests and scribes, and be killed, and be raised again the third day. Then Peter took Him, and began to rebuke

119

Him, saying, 'be it far from Thee, Lord: this shall not be unto Thee.' But He turned, and said unto Peter, *Get thee behind Me Satan: thou art an offence unto Me: for thou savourest not the things that be of God, but those that be of men.*" Yes, it is true that I will make even your enemies be at peace with you. There is a season for everything, and if you seem to escape the experience of learning through suffering, then ask yourself if you really are in My will.

Once the Holy Spirit comes into your life through your commitment, He just doesn't leave it. That is because to your grave, He will continually strive to direct you *to the Word*. He will continue to be faithful even if and when you are not. The Word is different; He cannot dwell with you unless *you put Him in there*. And you must have Him within your heart and mind through *experiencing* the meat of the Word in your life. Ask yourself, how can the Holy Spirit bring the Word to your remembrance when you need Jesus to defend you, to protect you, to direct you? How?

Noah preached up until the flood came. Matthew 24:37-42 says, "But as the days of Noah were, so shall also the coming of the Son of man be. For as in the days that were before the flood they were eating and drinking, marrying and giving in marriage, until the day that Noe entered into the ark, And knew not until the flood came, and took them all away; so shall also the coming of the Son of man be. Then shall two be in the field; the one shall be taken, and the other left. Two women shall be grinding at the mill; the one shall be taken, and the other left. Watch therefore: for ye know not what hour your Lord doth come." Tell Me, do you honestly believe that I will take you if you never truly committed yourself *to the Word* the way I intended? Do you honestly believe that I will be able to get your attention at that moment when I could not get your attention all this time? If Jesus Christ holds such little interest for you now, how will you hear Him then?

If your focus right now is to the earth, it will be to the earth then. I Am telling you now that the day will come when it dawns on people that they need to get serious about their commitment to the Word, and it may be too late. They will run to do "catch-up" and not be able to. Just before it happens like a lightning flash across the sky, the truth will be revealed to every soul that claimed Me. And there will be those who trusted in their gift to save them, and they put off the Word and put off their commitment, and they will be shocked. I explained what I meant by trusting in your own works. Some are gifted for those works, but that is not what saves you. *I Am giving you the greatest warning of your life.* No matter who you are, what you do, what you say, how good you are at it, it means nothing because you need to be completely committed in the Word. Then the Holy Spirit can work with Me as one within you. Abide in Me and I in you. How can Jesus abide on the shelf put off so that you can do your will today? Today is the day of salvation. Matthew 24:44 (KJV) says, "Therefore be ye also ready: for in such an hour as ye think not the Son of man cometh." How can I write My Word on the fleshy tables of your heart when you don't know what it says? Why? Because you let someone tell you and trust in the fact that they know? *How foolish!*

The five foolish virgins needed the anointing that can only come in knowing the Word as part of their life with the Holy Spirit given at conversion. They were pure; they did not permit the world, the flesh, or the devil to touch them. *Yet they did not enter in. They can only trim their lamps with the anointing of the Son and the Holy Spirit.* There is so much preaching on the Holy Spirit and not enough preaching on Jesus Christ which is the Word, and *you need both in order to do My will.* When you experience the Living Word through the presence of the Holy Spirit within you, the *enemy can never steal it from you. It remains within you forever because you have experienced the truth.* Somebody didn't tell it to you, you did not simply just read it, and you did not force it into you. You allowed God to operate within you through His word. No one can steal it. Revelation can be forgotten, and you can even let it slip. Experiencing the Word within you can never be stolen. You have heard that you need that personal experience. But you have heard it as though it is a one-time thing that you do when you give your life to Christ. That one-time experience was to continue as you work out your salvation with fear and trembling. It is a daily, all-day-long experience until it is time to meet Me.

Just as I sent John the Baptist to prepare the way for the coming of My Son, I will also send those to preach and teach the truth to prepare the hearts and minds of those who are Mine for the rapture. It is the time and the hour to be prepared. Take the Word to your hearts. Permit the Holy Spirit to reveal to you how to operate according to His will, not your will. Remember I promised in My word to be to you according to what you are to Me. Psalm 18:25, 26 (KJV) says, "With the merciful Thou wilt shew Thyself merciful; with an upright man Thou wilt shew Thyself upright; with the pure Thou wilt shew Thyself pure; and with the forward Thou wilt shew Thyself forward." Remember when you are determined to have your will and your way with My Son, I will be determined to have My will and My way with you.

Anyone can see the time just before Jesus calls His church. The hour is obvious to anyone who has eyes or ears. Ask yourself a question, how much preaching have you heard about this? When the truth is preached around the world and people are taught the truth. I do not mean taking *part* of the truth to make money or keep your congregations. I Am talking about drawing the obedient to your ministries by being obedient enough to preach and teach absolute obedience to the Word in all things. I Am speaking about teaching and preaching that the Word must be imparted into your heart and mind through *experiencing absolute obedience through the things that you suffer.* All of those aspects that are now being taught about Me are definitely of Me. Using only those aspects to obtain what you so desire is *not* of Me. Preaching and teaching them without ever emphasizing the truths spoken here are not all right. The basics of salvation have been lost. True discipleship is obsolete within any and all churches. Discipleship is the first thing that needs to be done to cause someone to *let God abide in them through the Word.*

PART XI

"Love never faileth: but whether there be prophecies, they shall fail; whether there be tongues, they shall cease; whether there be knowledge, it shall vanish away. For we know in part, and we prophesy in part. But when that which is perfect is come, then *that which is in part shall be done away. When I was a child, I spake as a child, I understood as a child, I thought as a child: but when I became a man, I put away childish things. For now we see through a glass, darkly; but then face to face: now I know in part; but then shall I know even as also I am known. And now abideth faith, hope and love, these three: but the greatest of these is love*" (1 Corinthians 13:8-13).

*T*he Bible is a mirror; it is the Word that reflects exactly who you are *to yourself.* If you have rose-colored glasses on, you will never see yourself in it as you are. If you desire to do so, you can clearly see what you are doing or what you are not doing. It is as plain as the nose on your face. That reflection is designed to cause you to be led to repentance, to cause you to live what you read. Not to gloss over, pass over, or say to yourself that is not for you; and never did I mean it for you. You even say that the Word doesn't specifically say this or that in our time, so I Am saying this or that in our time *now.*

I Am not speaking about prophesying so that you can be seen or heard and thought of as the greatest prophet or your prophecies tickle the ears of those who support you. I Am speaking of telling the truth. If a man does wrong, he has consequences. If he makes mistakes in judgment and you tell others to let it go, you are not of Me. Because that man needs to be warned, and he needs to realize that simply telling him that I will let it go has no value to his soul, only to his physical desires and needs. Those choices of judgment are too important considering the things which he pursues. I cannot help him if you help Him against Me and make Me look as though I am harping on something that needs to be brought out in the light and needs to be dealt with by him. You may believe that I Am unfair. Read My Word again. Responsibility of the shallow degree of understanding for the word that you do have can benefit you only with those you comfort. As a prophet, you may have a tremendous gift, but if you have not endured living the word to the fullest extent, then you have no true prophecy. It may come out the way you have said it, but did it bring the truth that the Spirit of Truth desires to be brought forth? *If it doesn't cause a soul to repent, then you are comforting someone who needs correction.* I promise you that if this vessel who wrote this book has paid a price in understanding to tell the truth and you are bold enough to rebuke her openly, I may let you do it, and she may not even care what you think. Your thinking has turned into believing that love means that you must hate someone or something because of the way you think things are. Yes, at the end of all things, you will have to face Me with it. You may face Me today with it. And I Am not speaking of taking you.

This hour upon the church is too important for Me to have to choose between one or the other because you fancy yourself to be more than you are. Those who need the truth hang in the balance. There are those right now who are very sincere, who love Me very much and have never heard the truth. They cannot even see it because someone stands there, comforting them when they need to be dealt with. My sheep will hear My voice, and they will run from someone who will not tell them the truth.

I Am not writing this to say that everyone who is looking for God to come and deliver them will not see Me. I Am saying that those who seem to obtain through lies, through deceptions, and seem to take advantage will not meet Me with any joy. Many will say have they not done many wonderful works in My name, and I will say, "Depart from Me ye that work iniquity, I never knew you." The works of hatred for any men, hatred for white, hatred for black, hatred for red, hatred for yellow, hatred for brown, hatred for even blue is *not of Me.* You can say it is, you can pray it is, you can gainsay it is, but I repeat, *I join in no cause that puts brother against brother. All of you are My creation, and I have told you that they will know you are Christians by your love for the brethren. The brethren are those who live My Word.* Some of you are so deceived into believing that love means that you must hate someone or something because of the way you think things are. Yes, I hate oppression; yes, I hate sin. But I did not fight any of these things with Satan's tools. Once you pick up a cause to obtain what you think I want, you are on your own. And woe unto you if you seem to obtain it, for that only convinces you that you are right when you are wrong. Therefore, My promise to all who do not have the love of the truth is to send strong delusion. This was done so that you would believe a lie because you love not the truth. Are you deluded? How many times will I have to tell you to examine yourselves, see if you are reprobate? Do you not know what I meant? Are you so far gone that you cannot see? To be reprobate means I give you up to what you think, what you want, what you desire, what you feel, in other words, what you lust after.

The gospel of hatred for anyone who is made in My image that is preached in some churches is not of Me. Read Matthew and see what I said about being angry with someone without a cause. Because your ancestors suffered through the hand of someone else, and you feel that you deserve more, is not reason to hate everyone that has more than you. Why didn't you simply glorify Me and work until you obtained what you desired? You say you had no chance, and how everyone was against you? But then that is why I left you My Word, My Name, and My Spirit for you to overcome. And no man, no woman who has ever put My Son's Word in their heart and mind would have failed; you will see that all that is not of Me fails. Doesn't that tell you something? But it is easier to force, easier to steal, easier to fight, and in the end you lose and blame everyone else.

I appeal to you even now to remember that in Luke chapter 9 when the disciples of Jesus asked Him if He wanted them to call down fire from heaven to destroy the Samaritans for not believing in Him, He said that the Son of man came not to destroy, but to save. Jesus came to save, to heal, to deliver, and to set souls free. *Not to give them power to hate and blame all their problems on everyone else but themselves.* You say that you have no opportunities because of unrighteous men. I would have made a way long time ago had you not listened to the voice of hatred. You say that no one cared. I cared until I saw you seek out ways to destroy. *I commanded you to hate sin in you first.* I never did lead anybody to hate another.

There are those in this nation that have not dirtied their hands, who have not dirtied their hearts and minds with the world and the things of this world. They are precious to Me. But if they have engaged in one unrighteous act, they will have to go before Me and ask for forgiveness and make things right. You are no different. You are not permitted to have bitterness in your heart for any reason. Are you bitter because you cannot obtain what you so desire for yourself or for another? Do you bite off your nose to spite your face? You are not anyone's judge. I called you to judge *you* so that no one can judge you. You have such a huge beam in your eye, and you are so filled with the hatred that you listen to lies saying that hating the country you were born into is by My design. You believe that hating the people who have more than you is somehow My design. If this nation seems to have done you wrong, it is because you and your leaders never did obey My Word and pray for this country the way I instructed you to do and not against it. I commanded it to be so, and when I speak of leaders, I Am speaking of your church leaders.

I find no fault with those who are used by Me to bring out the truth and stand up for it. How will you know which one is which? How will you know the difference between a liar and an honest person? It is easy. Those who love Me could never destroy the innocent for any reason. Those who love Me could never give the power to destroy a helpless innocent individual to any man or any woman. You will know them by their fruits. I have seen those who are able to stand before you as though they are some great savior, and their power to persuade casts a spell on its audience. I tell you now, I hold the truth in My Word. You will know them by their fruits. And if anyone tells you that they are not answerable for making the choice to help someone destroy an innocent baby, decide now whom you will believe. Choose you this day whom you will serve.

Don't you realize that love is an act of your own free will? And so is hatred. *You choose* the power and the presence of good or bad by your own free will. To love or to hate someone or something is all a matter of choice. *Fear* of never obtaining, fear of being taken advantage of, fear of the unknown, fear of anything or anyone, is the absolute root of hatred. Fear someone else will obtain, fear that something will happen because of someone, fear even that your child or your family will suffer—all is the root, and the call of Satan to help you drive your children drives others to obtain. And eventually that fear turns into hatred; and eventually you become so frustrated, so angry that you cannot remember why you are fearful, why you are so hateful. You only know that you do, and you keep on refusing to let it all go and forgive and believe rather than to be afraid.

While it is true that our enemies hate us more than some of you love your country, they also fear this country first, that is why they hate us. It isn't your arrogance, it isn't anything but their fear that you will obtain what they do not want anyone to obtain, and therefore they hate you. That fear birthed the worst hatred this world has ever seen. How different are you than they? They took the Bible and took out what they wanted out of it. Made their own religion and called it by their own name and fed it even to children to hate and kill. They took Jesus out of the principles that began with Him and made them into what they wanted. And because you do it in a church that is called Christian, you think you are better than those who openly hate Me. As I said before, they have a better chance because when they hear the truth, they can and do get saved because I Am able to reveal to them who they really are. But you are more difficult because you have so much to say that you are Mine when you are not.

When a white man holds a person of any color down, he is doing evil. He can claim Me all he wants, but the presence of hatred is clear and evident. He becomes a liar on top of everything else when he goes to the church and claims to be a Christian. When a black man or a white man deliberately speaks out with words of hatred, he is no different. He has become the very thing that he hates, the very thing he is pointing out as though it belongs to the other. Both are wrong. Once any one of you opens your mouth to speak words of hatred for any race, to make fun of it, to mock it, and to speak against any country let alone your own, you become what you hate. This is why I hate gainsaying, this is why I hate gossip, and this is why I hate things to fester in secret. This is why I hate those filthy rags of gossip. The heart is exceedingly wicked above all things.

I Am not offended by those who stand up and speak the truth in My Word. I Am not offended by those who tell it like it is. I Am not offended by those who do not twist and turn My Word to make it sound the way they want.

I Am offended by those who draw the ignorant, those who take advantage of people who do not know what is really going on. I hate to see so many young people or people who don't speak English or people who cannot read drawn in by a pied piper because he looks so good and he sounds so good and he is willing to gather up all those who have no idea of what life is all about. This kind of person is capable of anything to get ahead. That is taking advantage of the young, the poor, and the ignorant. To make fun out of the elderly who deserve your respect and encourage them to pick on those who are older is very displeasing to Me. Waken up, My children, those of you who are older. Understand if they can tear one man down because he is older, they have no real concern to help the elderly of this nation. And you need to be concerned in this nation about what they intend to do with the elderly. The wisdom that comes from experience is worth its weight in gold. *I ordained it to be so. Hear Me!*

The vessel writing this book has had so many things against her, so many ways to hurt her, and she understands that her life is *exactly what she makes it. She hated and fought against no one, blamed no one who ever caused her heartache or pain, and she did not cry, "Poor me," because she was born in poverty.* She is thankful because all of it caused her to recognize Me, and it caused her to see love for the first time in her life. Caused her to see that she is forgiven for all, and that means she is to forgive all. She wasn't always like that, but she allowed Jesus to live within her enough to become like that, and this is how she lives today. Some of you strive to live like this, so do other religions, but you leave out the Word, you insult My Son by taking what He taught as though it is your thoughts and understanding, worse yet as though they are the thoughts of your church leaders. The very fact that you leave His name out of your books, out of your teaching, tells Me plainly that you have rejected Him.

Let me ask you, how do you part from these basic principles in My church? A church called by My Name? The gospel is a message of repentance and forgiveness, and it takes love to live and think like that. What fruits are you growing? You, who listen to those who preach and teach hatred, remember My Word says that resentment and bitterness will defile many. What fruits are your leaders bearing? Oh, they seem to treat you good; therefore, you give your all to them, and you somehow do not see that they hold you with a fear that says if you don't agree with them, you are not of Me. I tell you here and now, if you listen to them, you are *not* listening to Me. When you go out into the world for anything, and the first thing that comes to your mind is that someone at your church or your preacher would not approve if you do or say certain things or wear your hair a certain way or wear certain things, and if they won't let you talk to anyone about the things they teach and preach in secret, *none* of it is of Me. If you have to have their approval to sit with certain people or go only certain places, they are not of Me. This is how Jesus was treated when he sat with the sinners and ate with them. Oh, they convince you that they treat you good; but if you were to use your own head and read the word on your own, you would see that they are wearing mink coats when you give all you have, they are in big cars and million-dollar estates while you live in poverty or close to it. Your hard-earned pennies did not go to Me, it went to them. Wake up and see; take off your rose-colored glasses. And when and where you see this is true, say nothing to anyone; never speak about it to no one but Me. Leave it all in My hands and seek someone who will tell you the truth. That truth is to overcome evil with good. That truth is to hate no one, envy no one, and covet no one's goods. If you make a decision to not follow them anymore, please help yourself and tell no one and fight no one. So that no one can accuse you of anything except that you no longer believe. And that is not a sin because I did not say that you had to believe and accept anyone simply because they claim to have Me in their heart. You are entitled to check out their fruits. They take advantage of the poor in spirit those who do not have enough to discern the truth for whatever reason.

PART XII

"And go, get thee to them of the captivity, unto the children of thy people, and speak unto them, and tell them, Thus saith the Lord GOD: whether they will hear, or whether they will forbear" (Ezekiel 3:11).

Listen to what I say, I urge you to understand. There are people who woo young people, perhaps female college students that leave home and have mothers and fathers just like you. These students get under the influence of those who consider themselves intelligent, and they are so vulnerable to worship anyone. These children are going through a stage of discovery. Some can come out of it, and some never do. Some never come out of throwing away what they have been taught all their life. These young girls that are exploited should be told by *any* older man who is the target of them saying that he is sexy or find him or her even attractive should be rebuked or at least not supported by getting on the Internet with them. If you have children, would you want them doing this with someone else when they grow up? Does a man have to have his ego so fed that he doesn't care that it is someone else's daughter? Do you have to be liked so badly that you just smile and let it all take place without speaking out against it? If a woman does this, she is just as bad. To be a godly mother or father, you must see these things no matter how busy you are. If you say that your

131

children are important to you, then why don't you speak out against these things that matter to your children? For what you do will come upon them.

Have you never read the scripture that tells you that if you hurt one of these little ones who believe in Me it is better for a millstone to be tied around your neck and you be dropped into the deepest sea rather than hurt one of these little ones that believe in Me? If you are forty or fifty, remember a girl of nineteen and twenty is just that, a little girl. Young ladies need to be taught how to protect these emotions and not give them out to everyone. Celebrities take advantage of them by the millions. Stars do not care what happens to someone else's little girl, only theirs. If any of these girls, even one was raised in a Christian home, and they turn away with your approval, with your support as their teacher, professor, or someone in public office, or even movie stars, rock stars, then expect the scripture to fall upon you if you do not repent. When you draw a child away from the truth and think you are something because you are able to do so, remember they belong to Me. I Am not warning one person. If you put a name to anyone spoken about here, that is your problem then, for I have not mentioned anyone. I Am speaking to all men, all women who do these things. And many of you do, do these things. If there is within you disrespect for someone's daughter or son, then how do you expect your children to be protected? But when you willfully and deliberately touch someone's children that belong to Me, you need to take heed to the fact that I keep good records. You need to hear testimonies of women or men in their eighties still loving and honoring their professors out of college, or their teachers, or whatever because they led them out of church; they led them out of My will and convinced them into an alternative lifestyle or convinced them into believing that the Word is nothing.

Paul in his day spoke of those who had no other concern except their bellies. Inside a person dwells a wolf when he rips and tears apart anyone who disagrees with him. There is nothing wrong in standing up for the truth and taking a firm stand if you are a prophet and God revealed something to you personally. But more than ever before, there are those who take what others have had revealed to them by God and do exactly what they do with the Bible. They take only that which they think can promote their ministry, their desires, their wants, and their needs. And although they sound so good, they will literally rip you apart. Not openly, for they are cowards. But secretly, in their closet of prayer that is filled with sin. For the first principles of right and wrong has slipped from their fingers. Thinking that gain is godliness, and because they have been able to obtain millions, they take it as though they have it all and how dare anyone go against them. That is why I labored to find a vessel that would know exactly how not to allow anyone no matter how great they seemed to be, persuade her out of the things that I have called her to tell. Once I tell her something, it is sealed in her heart and in her mind to such a degree that nothing and no one can make her doubt or back up when I have called her forward.

Now at first when I spoke to her her knowledge of words was limited, her abilities were limited, and therefore she came out with a raw manuscript. And just as the Bible seems to change as you grow, so does the message written in her seem to change. All messages to a prophet are filtered through their knowledge, their understanding, and their knowledge of even the language they are speaking. Their messages are filtered through their countries, their states. That is why I say that to have a message in this country cannot come from someone who claims to be a prophet from another country. It is impossible. When they get more educated, then the message is perfected. This is also true for different countries and states that you receive according to your experience and knowledge of what you have been through in understanding. Never think that I will call you to know anything in this country above those who are Mine in it. Never believe that I would reveal something to you to correct Mine when I Am able to keep them from falling. Why would I give any truth about this country and its leadership to anyone who was not born and raised in this country? For only in that can I work with them in understanding enough to do the job in the country. Some of you cross over in your pride and ignorance of what this is all about.

There are things that are written within the pages of this book that a lot of people would like to leave it unsaid. But if she takes heed to

133

you and leaves them unsaid, then she is not in My will. What makes manifest is the light. That statement is greater than any one person who thinks they know something that they know nothing about. Had I called any vessel to work out their own salvation with fear and trembling and they were able to hear My voice, they could not deny the truth. I deliberately gave her a list of people to send her manuscript to. I told her plainly that those who had the Holy Spirit, that those who knew Me and taught the truth would respond favorably. I revealed to her that there would be those who would recognize the Word of God in this book. And there were only six that even responded. Only three responded favorably, and there were those who took what they wanted out of what they read and turned it to work for them and not for Me. We will see who are Mine, I told her. We will know which ones are which. If I give a message of My Spirit and someone denies or rejects it, I Am not saying that they do not have My Spirit, I Am only saying they are not where they need to be in love.

Every person that was sent a manuscript went into prayer, and she felt each one's response in the Spirit before they ever responded with a letter.

In writing some of the things that I revealed to her, the demonic forces manifested themselves before her. She was totally encased within My Presence that the moment these forces appeared, they had to leave; they trembled before her, for none can stand in My Presence. At one point, I told her that they were sent because she dared to speak the truth. *Matthew 10:26-28 (KJV) says, "Fear them not therefore; for there is nothing covered, that shall not be revealed; and hid, that shall not be known. What I tell you in darkness that speak ye in light: and what ye hear in the ear, that preach ye upon the housetops. And fear not them which kill the body, but are not able to kill the soul: but rather fear Him which is able to destroy both soul and body in hell."* She made a decision led by My Spirit to take certain things out of her manuscript, not due to fear, not due to making a mistake but because I revealed to her that once it was read by someone who has that ministry, it is now *their* responsibility to do something about what they read.

Matthew 7:21-23 (KJV) says, "Not every one that saith unto Me, Lord, Lord, shall enter into the kingdom of heaven; but he that doeth the will of My Father which is in heaven. Many will say to Me in that day, Lord, Lord, have we not prophesied in Thy name? And in Thy name have cast out devils? And in Thy name done many wonderful works? And then will I profess unto them, I never knew you: depart from me, ye that work iniquity." These works that He speaks of are not and never were evil. These are the very works that He did. Those who trust in their gifts, those who trust in what I have used them for instead of trusting in Jesus, will not hear Me when I call. They simply will think they are rebuking the devil for they have no idea as they live each and every day that they are resting in, trusting in their abilities, their gifts, and not in Christ. Worse yet, they carry it so far that they depend on it at the judgment enough to confess those are the things that saved them. It never occurred to them that although I called them, although I gifted them, although they prophesied over millions, although they cast out devil for millions, and although each and every day they did many wonderful works, they forgot that those things have not the power to save them; all those things are not the reason they get into heaven. Many will be lost way out of course simply because they puff themselves up too highly and forget that *Jesus is the only way into heaven. They forget that Jesus is the Word and I value My Word above all that I gave you to do and all that I did with you. For when you toss Him aside, you toss the cross aside, and that is the only way you can destroy your own soul. So the very works that Jesus did become sin to you, because you did not protect yourself and ask Jesus to work it all out as to why you do these things. Pride goeth before a fall.*

What I wrote in My Word will stand forever. How can you permit anyone to take what I have said and make it what they want? How is it that if someone comes in their own name, you will receive them, but you will not receive someone who has the approval of God? John 5:39-44 says, "Search the scriptures; for in them ye think ye have eternal life: and they are they which testify of Me. And ye will not come to Me, that ye might have life. I receive not honor from men. But I know you, that ye have not the love of God in you. I am come in My Father's name,

135

and ye receive Me not: if another shall come in his own name, him ye will receive. How can ye believe, which receive honor one of another, and seek not the honor that cometh from God only."

How do you separate the scriptures to suit yourselves and listen to those who tell you what they say that it says? It is plainly written for centuries in red so that you may know exactly what Jesus said. And yet you go directly against those words because of the teachings of man. They teach traditions. Those traditions erase my commandments. Has it ever occurred to you that I thought it not good for man to be alone therefore I sent him Eve? From the very beginning, I ordained it that way, and then someone comes along and tells you that if you want to be used in the church you cannot marry. Can you not see that when you turn off natural affections you leave the door open to unnatural affections? You wonder why this has hit the church. So many of you cry out and wonder why this has happened in your churches. Yet you never go into the Word to read what I had to say about these things. You continually let everyone else tell you. If and when men are permitted to marry, if and when women are permitted to marry, there is no room for the enemy to take advantage and cause these things to be. Paul said it is better to marry than to burn. You can burn with lust and burn eternally for it if you do not repent.

Romans 1:25 says, "Who changed the truth of God into a lie, and worshipped and served the creature more than the Creator, who is blessed forever. Amen." When you lift up *any* man higher than God and give him the power to be in the place of God and permit him to tell you things that go directly against the Words written by Jesus Christ, that is lifting up the creature and serving him more than the Me, the Creator. How can anyone on one hand do what they are told by someone else and on the other hand deny what My Word says *and all the while claiming to be Mine, claiming to have guidance from the Word?* Can you not see that this isn't even close to My intentions? I am not like you. I will not change My mind, nor will I ever turn from My Word. Please consider all the things that I am striving to tell you because the day will come when I will literally lift what you seem to have from you. And in that moment you will know that I am not with you, and in that day you will turn toward the truth, and you will want to work it all out with Me. Therefore, I sent this book to awaken you out of sleep, to awaken you out of those things that want to destroy you; and no matter how difficult it seems to get into My Word, I am calling you to read it for yourself. Discover it for yourself. Not as though you can open doors with some kind of combinations by using it to obtain what you want or desire. This day for My church is ending. This misuse of My Word is ending. I appeal to you as someone that I love very much that you get into the Word and pray that you be found worthy through obedience. The lack of willingness to suffer daily the cross only seems to be something that you do. Because you have lived so deliciously, you have no idea that there is so much more to it than where you have gone and what you seem to be doing. I am not a man that I change My mind and say one thing and mean another. Much of My Word is written very plainly. Through the Presence and power of My Holy Spirit, there is nothing in My Word that is hard to understand. All you have to do is ask for My Spirit to lead you into all truth as I have promised that I would.

I ask you a question. You who do these things and refuse to repent, how do you say you have any love? How do you sleep at night and feel so safe that no harm will come when you do so much harm to others?

PART XIII

"And He answered and said unto them, Have ye not read, that He which made them at the beginning made them male and female, And said, For this cause shall a man leave father and mother, and shall cleave to his wife: and they twain shall be one flesh? Wherefore they are no more twain, but one flesh. *What therefore God hath joined together, let not man put asunder.* They say unto Him, Why did Moses then command to give a writing of divorcement, and to put her away? He saith unto them, Moses *because of the hardness of your hearts* suffered you to put away your wives: but from the beginning it was not so" (Matthew 19:4-8).

To teach submission, to teach that man is head of the house is not evil, for it is clearly in My Word. But to teach it simply because it says so without any understanding is like teaching a child to behave themselves without ever giving them understanding as to why they should. And because of this, many have some of the Word but do not clearly understand the importance of why I made it so.

Your spouse is a reflection of yourself. You say it is not so. Surely it cannot be true because he or she is doing this or saying that and I Am the only one here who is right, the only one who is holy and the

138

only faithful and true one. This statement proves to Me that you are not what and who you say you are. My commandment was to *let* no man put asunder what I have joined together. And that means you. If in Corinthians I told you that his body is not his and her body is not hers and they belong to the other spouse, I did not mean simply where sex was concerned. Although many of you apply it only there and think that you are doing Me a favor in your sacrificial obedience. Both sides do this, not just a man and not just a woman, but both sides do this.

You see the scripture says that your spouse is sanctified by your faith, which means they are set apart to be made holy. And yet you hear them curse and swear, you hear them scream and yell, you hear them lie on you and perhaps in some cases call you names. You see them at the drop of a hat rail at you, get irritated and frustrated, and take their problems out on you. And because you see all of this, you become convinced that they are the sinner and you are the saint. And so since the scripture doesn't seem to fit the situation, you in some cases are sure they are headed for hell and you are for heaven. In believing this, you have just put your marriage asunder. To put something asunder, you must break it in pieces, separate it. And your spouse is part of your body because you are no more twain but one. But you ignore that part because it doesn't please your flesh, and the other way to see the truth is just too hard. This is where some of you will get angry and tell Me that the vessel who wrote this never endured what you have to go through. There is no way that she could understand and that poor you, she never lived with you.

Up until now, you have only been able to see your spouse's hardened heart. You have never taken a good look at yours. Two are always tempted especially when they are one. The enemy of your soul attacks you where you are the most vulnerable. And you could see clearly where your spouse is, but you cannot see clearly where you are. You are exactly where you *think* they are. Remember they are a reflection of you. Your rose-colored glasses are on. They make everything rosy for you, and you are leaving nothing for the other because you have already in your heart cut them off. And the end of this road is divorce. It just doesn't matter to you that they are the other half of your body. You only know your pain, and you never see theirs; and when you do see it, you say to yourself that they deserve it, that they asked for it. And you fully expect Me to not see your part in all of this, for Me not to see how much you contributed to the situation. You can apply the negative of the Word to them, but not to you.

Let's look at all of it the way it really is, because if you don't see it without your rosy glasses, you will always have to live with yourself, and you may wind up alone. If I send you a good person into your life, you would destroy them the way you helped to destroy this one. If your right arm suddenly had a mind of its own and did its own thing and swung around uncontrollably, would you cut it off? And if you did cut it off, would you not bleed for a while? And would you not be so sore and hurt because now you have no arm and you will never be the same without it? No matter how it heals, it will always be gone. So you will be handicapped and hindered. Now don't twist and turn this to mean that I Am speaking about you not leaving a person who abuses you or sexually abuses your children or does some other damage to you or your children. I did give you a way out for the adulterer that they not bring home a disease. I did give you a way out with someone that it is impossible to get along with. I told you to separate but to stay unmarried. Why do you think I would say that? I'll tell you why because I know that if you leave with the attitude that you made no mistakes, that the spouse is the only one to blame, you will do worse the second time around. So it is better to remain unmarried rather than to destroy another. And that if you part, My Word says that if it is done simply to have fornication with someone, then you cause your spouse to commit adultery if they remarry. Hard to understand, isn't it? No harder than salvation. I have an answer to everything; if you look for it in My Word, you will find it.

If your arm acted up, more than likely you would take it to your heart, hold it close to you, bind a bandage on it to keep it in place, and put something on it to soothe it, nurse it, take care of it, and be kind to it. You would actually baby it and not use it until it is healed. All those things would be done to that part of your body. You would even carry it around in a sling if you had to. *But never with your own hand would you hurt yourself so badly that you would cut it off. After all, it is a member of your body and you need it.*

A man cannot easily express how he feels, and sometimes he doesn't even know how he feels. If he is a good man, he will be a good provider, he will take care of you when you are sick, and he will do what is needed. This vessel who wrote this book married a good man. Because of her not being a Christian, because she did not know what salvation was, nor ever heard of it until she was thirty-one years old, their marriage began in trouble. Believe Me, she did as much as he did to destroy their marriage. But when she became a Christian, things changed. She then saw him as someone that I died for. That made everything different. Do you see your spouse as someone that I paid a great price for? Look at them again.

Seeing him this way caused her to constantly renew her vows no matter what her flesh said. No matter how much she wanted to please her flesh, she denied herself and worked at her marriage to be obedient to Me. One day I told her to sit down and make a list of all the good and all the bad about him. When she did, she discovered that what she thought was bad about him was nothing more than her selfish desires. When she cut off the selfishness, she was left with a lot of good about him. As a matter of fact, today she is very grateful and thankful that she has him as her husband. She looks at him now and sees all the reasons why she fell in love with him and married him. She feels fortunate that they are still there, and she did not destroy those attributes with her mouth.

She would get displeased with him and say things like "You're mean" or "You're rotten." And one day I asked her, why doesn't she use her tongue to speak good over him? She chose to love him. She made a commitment to Me to keep her marriage vows and love him, trusting in Me that she would reap what she sowed. If you sow love, you will reap love; sow respect, you reap respect; sow honor, you reap honor. If you sow the opposite, you will reap the opposite.

Someone gave her a book that taught to fascinate him. And she threw the book away because she refused to pretend, to manipulate his feelings, and to take his manhood away from him by deceiving him with fascination. She said, "Lord, You never fascinated anyone. You were who You were, and You did not act, nor did you pretend." She simply refused to be anything but honest and loving to him. Their marriage lasted, going on forty-five years. And she loves him more than she ever did before. Why? Obedience. She respects him more than she ever has. Why? Obedience. She doesn't see herself making some great sacrifice as though she is the only one in this house who has God. She sees his importance to Me. She is careful to submit and obey that My Word be not blasphemed.

Her husband trusts her, and her daughter in her own language calls her blessed. Both of them do not believe like she does. But she no longer kicks against where she is. She no longer has to endure the pain. You see, she knows how powerful the blood of Jesus is, and she safely trusts in Me. She understands that only I convert the soul. She sees no reason to argue, fight, and strive to convince anyone of sin. She understands that is the job of My Holy Spirit to convict. She understands that it is My choice of when and what to do. And until I do the operation, it simply will not happen. So she sees no need to cry or beg or plead. She sees no reason to hurt. She is perfectly content exactly where she is in life because she has Me. Godliness with contentment is great gain. And she has peace within her home while she waits on Me. I called her and you to peace.

When she would get tempted to plunge into the argument in the flesh, she would run to her secret place and tell him and Me that she is not leaving this room until she comes out a Christian. And with that, she would pray until she felt My Presence and then humbly come out and apologize for any little part of it and tell him that he is responsible for himself toward God and what they went through wasn't one sided, both were wrong, and she would be sorry enough to repent. Her immediate prayer is "I forgive" always.

Your belief system has power to enable the enemy of your soul to have a field day within your home. You give him all he needs as long as you are so silly that you think you are the only one who has God. If I sanctified the spouse, I set them apart to make them holy. So many times she would tell Me that she believes that the scripture is true.

I could tell you many more things, but I want you to know that this country has so many people getting divorced, and they can't get along, and many times the one who thinks they are so godly is the very one who has the door open for the enemy to take over. Worse yet, they are received by most churches simply because they attend. Never mind that the other side is never spoken, never mind that the one who isn't attending has no say to defend themselves. One should never be received unless it is adultery, unless it is abuse, even mental and emotional abuse or verbal abuse; but then you need to investigate it in prayer whether it is true or not. Someone could walk into your church and be filled with the Spirit and still be mistaken, because all of you are capable of making mistakes.

In the beginning when I first dealt with her, I would warn her not to do the things so many of you do. I revealed to her in My fear that if she continued, she would be very sorry. The fear, the respect for My Word kept her from making many terrible mistakes. Her ability to reach so many is simply because she has led every thought captive to Christ by allowing Jesus to live within her and not her own selfish desires and whims. When she got tempted to believe that her spouse would never appreciate all she was doing, and believe Me, she strove hard to obey, I told her plainly, "Don't do it for him; do all things for Me. He may never appreciate you, but I will and I do." From that time on, she has never complained about what he thinks, feels, says, or does; she does all things for Me, and she kept her love for him intact. She knows that love has nothing to do with how you are treated, what is said, or what is done. And I was not speaking about her going around him as though she has an upper edge. Or faking humility in or to see him hurt or cursed. I Am speaking about her having sincere forgiveness and repentance on her part because she believes that love is love, it is unselfish, and it is everything that Corinthians 13 says it is. That is her guide to loving everyone, not just him. She binds the word within her heart. And she has been blessed in seeing him grow within with the things that are of Me. According to his knowledge, I Am able to work with him.

When your spouse acts up or your children do, it is that God is manifesting something for you to understand and for you to see. You who are more spiritual to understand and for you to do something about it in prayer, if I wanted them dealt with, I would have come to you as a friend and would have told you that I Am going to deal with your spouse. In most cases, no one comes to Me; all they do is cry about a condition that I have revealed needs help, and because they are not where they need to be in the Spirit, they run with it in the flesh. And then no one gets any help, and most of all the disobedience of the so-called more spiritual one permits Satan to make Me look like I Am unwilling and unable. When all along the one unwilling and unable is the one who will not listen. Don't you understand that if your spouse is sanctified by your faith, that means that you are never to give in to believing that Satan has the power to overcome and overwhelm them with a foul spirit, a disobedient, contentious spirit? That means when God reveals to you their temptation to give in to such things, you are to pray for them *that they not be taken*. You are not to go cry for yourself and to others and become useless to Me in what I called you to do. You literally give them willingly up to Satan as though you are so much better because you see how hard you tried, never knowing that perhaps they tried with all they had. But because it isn't like you or like you think or according to what you feel, you desert them in prayer and separate yourself from your marriage. I called you to keep it together not these things or these ways. Is it so hard to understand that if Satan can touch the other half of you, he can and will touch you? When the problems begin to come, before they become overwhelming, you need to fight the problems in the Spirit; but that is the very thing that you don't fight. You don't fight Satan, but you do fight the other half of your body. You seem to be so spiritual to everyone else, but you're a baby when it comes to understanding your own body. You do not know how to possess your vessel.

Most of you are so tied to the flesh emotionally that you can't see past your own nose. If you would have only examined yourselves instead of examining the other and kept your mind off of My business. Your spouse's walk with God is between them and Me and none of your business. The only place you need is to be spiritually where you are to protect them from giving in to Satan. This is the *only* authority a man truly has in his marriage. That he be wise enough to see when his wife is being tempted in the flesh that he may protect her from Satan. Many of you are so puffed up, in desperate need to feed your own ego that you become a lord over your spouse and your children. You are driven by fear that you will lose your headship, afraid that you will somehow lose part of your manhood that you drive them with fear. Your prayers in your closet are filled with sin. As a wife and a mother from this kind of home, you drive your children with the fear that this might happen to them, and that might happen to them. And all of you don't ever trust or rest, nor do you believe that what you are doing is wrong. With your eyes always on what will the neighbors think, what will the pastor think, what will the church think, what will your family think? And this drives you even more to drive them. How do you think I overcame the world, by fighting it or by overcoming evil with evil? I overcame it with good. How can you be so much without wisdom on the simplest things? How can you run to people who claim My name and they be without wisdom when they hold your hand, sympathize with you, and feed the forces that are striving to destroy you and your family rather than save them?

Ask yourself, did I put you two together? Were you called, meaning did you become aware of your need to be reborn during your marriage? Because if you did, then I hold you to it and tell you don't desire to be unmarried and that your spouse is sanctified by your faith. But your failure in prayer falls upon you, and you endure untold hardship because you have separated in prayer. By believing that they are going to pay, and what you don't know is so are you! Did you get married knowingly in My Presence and make a commitment and a vow to love, honor, and obey your spouse? Did you commit yourself in sickness and in health, till death do you part? Then what you did was *in My Presence, and I joined you together*. Once you invite Me into the situation, I do My part. This is why I said, "What God has joined together let not man put asunder." You invite Me into the situation, but you don't want Me in the situation. You ask Me to help you and you tell yourself and Me that you are seeking Me and all the while you are fighting Me and seeking what you want. Does that make any sense to you? Then when things

145

become disappointing to you and you do not find the relationship that you pictured from the television or from the movies, when you find that this thing called happiness doesn't exist like that, then you go down in despair and depression. You feel so sorry for yourself, then you begin to lie to yourself and take it to others, and there you begin to defile many with your lies. You never realize how much you have allowed others in this world to form your thinking. How much you permitted the enemy of your soul to give you such an unrealistic view of what life and love are all about.

When you get married, you think that you are entering into a relationship that would cause some sort of utopia. And you are so unprepared for what life is all about even though you have gone through some kind of counseling to prepare you for marriage. The whole understanding of what love is about doesn't sink in where the *responsibility* to another is concerned. Your greatest commitment was to love; your greatest responsibility was to love. Without love, you have no respect. I watch men married to so-called spiritual women look up to their wives in their heart and know that these women have Me in them. These men labor to strive to please Me; and when they make a mistake, they immediately fall headlong down, down, down. They compare themselves to their wives because they do not understand they don't need to be like their wives, they need to be them. And the wife doesn't understand that they don't need to be like them, they need to be who they are in Me. Because they know they cannot be like the one they live with; and the wife, having more knowledge, looks on their mistakes as though they are going to pay. Then the husbands look at it as though they are going to pay. And they don't know how to turn to Me and ask Me, and the wife doesn't turn to Me and ask Me. They think they did, but all they did was blubber and complain and expect Me to pull something out and suit them with it. And so when they get up off of their knees, they feel better, and I still love them, and I witness that love to them, but I never witness against their spouse. I never witness that I Am against their spouse because I know they are ignorant. When My Spirit falls in these situations, you take it as though I Am for you and against them, and this is a lie. You took it that way because you assume that I would desert them the way you did. Then your husbands throw their hands up in the air and give up and tell themselves there is no hope, they are going to hell, so they might as well not try to please Me any more because *you* showed them that they can't. Because you cannot be pleased as long as you believe that you are so much better than them. Your mistakes do not seem as bad to you, but they equal out. Have you no wisdom? They are watching you thinking it is Me in you; and when you fail to be there to forgive them and lift them and let them know that even if it takes a million failures as long as they are willing to get back up and strive toward Me I will be with them and so will you, then they have a chance to be pulled out of the devil's snare because with you on My side to save them, working together, We can see them come to Jesus. But then again, this takes self-denial, dying daily to self, and that is all too much like work. It is easier to go on and fool yourselves, never understanding that your spouse is not really against you, you are. Satan cannot succeed unless you give him the power to do so. Nothing is worse than someone who believes they are right in Me when they are the opposite.

Sometimes for a while your dreams seemed to be fulfilled. Some of you stay within that unrealistic dream and refuse anything else that tells you the truth, and it ends tragically for you. You have some knowledge and understanding of what is expected of you as a husband or a wife, and you think that is enough to keep you and help you through thick and thin, through the good and the bad, and you wind up with only the bad and wonder why in the end and for years it still troubles you, asking yourself, "Why did it have to be this way? Why couldn't it have turned out better?" You get hurt because your spouse in secret is doing things they ought not because you were never close enough to Me to hear Me warn you or tell you what was taking place. Oh, I told you, I called you, but you were so wrapped up in yourself that you could not hear Me. And your children suffered, and all the blame looked like it was on the one who was doing all of it. Oh, if only you would have really been as spiritual as you claimed, you would have been able to put Satan in his place. But you were too busy putting the Word in its place. The cry within your heart is to not be alone. You are willing to pay any price not to be alone. And thinking like this in the back of your mind and in the depth of your heart is so very dangerous for you because it will always come out in the forefront of your eyes. And you will always be hurt. Your rose-colored glasses will speak to you, and you can't even begin to hear Me. So for some of you who are alone, it is better to be alone than to repeat what you have just been through.

Some of you when you made this commitment never intended to keep it. It was just words that you spoke because it was the right thing to do, because somewhere you have been told or taught this is what you do. You are not looking to make someone else happy, which in itself is unrealistic. You are seeking your own benefit, your own self-gain in whatever you are looking for in a spouse. You are actually seeking self-fulfillment, self-satisfaction, which is all self, self, self, which is the worst way that you could enter into a relationship of any kind, let alone a commitment like marriage that is supposed to last you the rest of your life here on earth.

Self-deception comes in so many forms. Being awake and watching and praying is one way to handle it all, but for you it seems all too late. You are to watch and pray to see to it that you do not fall into temptation. If you had the Word within you, you would have been equipped to handle this thing called love and keep it the way I intended. My Word says if you are married to not desire to be unmarried and if you are unmarried not to desire to be married. Unless it becomes so unbearable because the person is so abusive, then the scripture tells you to depart but not to remarry. People don't want to hear that because these things sound like *denying* yourself. This is the part of the scripture that tells you that your dream will never come to pass, and so you desire your self-seeking dream. And you try to picture the future and do not realize that self gets in your way. Self, even when you're married, blinds your eyes.

PART XIV

"And I, if I be lifted up from the earth, will draw all men unto Me"(John 12:32).

Many of you have probably heard that scripture millions of times in your life. You probably right now think you could tell Me a thing or two about it. Here is true understanding when it comes to what or who you lift up. As you know, Satan will send people to trouble you, and God will send people to bless you, knowing who is the problem. I can say if you stay close to Me, you won't be deceived. You all have a draw within your spirits. You don't understand it at least in the beginning, and you do not realize that *you draw who you are*. If you are insecure, you draw the insecure. If you are unbelieving, you draw the unbelieving. Did you ever notice that when you gossip, talk about others, all others will come and talk to you about others? But when you decide that you will never talk about anyone, no one would dare come to you to talk because they already know your response. They can feel that you would never talk about another person before they even approach you. If you are fearful, you seem to draw the fearful. The intellectual draw the intellectual, and the foolish draw the foolish. The selfish draw the selfish. Each one feeds the other. The godly will draw the godly. Everyone who is looking for Jesus Christ the way that He is, not the way you make Him out to be, will be drawn to the truth. Some of you pay too much attention to those who do not want it when they come into your lives. Don't trouble, either they listen or they don't. And if they listen, they learn and change, and if they don't, they won't come around, and it is actually easier for you because you don't have to take them on as a responsibility. Conversion is what I work on in the Spirit, not you. It is the job of the Holy Spirit to convince people, not you.

You say, what does all of this have to do with lifting up Jesus? Well, just as you cannot deceive a child, you cannot continually deceive anybody who knows the Word and has the Holy Spirit. Just as you cannot pretend love to those who are less fortunate in their thinking, you cannot fool or deceive anybody. They will feel exactly where you are. Unless they are just like you, self-deceived. Then you truly have the blind leading the blind. People draw away from you when they feel your sincerity in the truth if they don't want it. People will draw away from you if they can feel that self-deception or that hidden desire to get them into your church. You know, for the numbers, to be seen as something that you are not. You wonder why many don't come. The main reason is that My Son is not lifted up within you.

If you put Jesus on the shelf and make Him stay in His place. Because as you put the Word in its place, you are telling Jesus to just stay in His place every time you refuse to read Him. If He was walking on the earth today, you would be telling Him exactly where He belongs in your life to you. Now how is that lifting Him up?

Picture this: you are a parent that loves your children. You can't wait to be with them, have them share part of themselves with you. You can't wait to go places and do things with them. You long to hold them and tell them and teach them all the things that you know are good for them. They get up in the morning, and they simply ignore you as though you are not there. They never talk to you, never look at you. It is as though you are invisible. They want nothing to do with you; they don't want to hear what you have to say. To them, what you have to say and what you think is so valueless. And although you wrote it all down in the hopes they would read it, still they ignore it after you went through so much to prepare it. And even though you wrote so much to keep them from hurting themselves, though you made every sacrifice with your life even, they still ignore you. They pass by you in the kitchen, pass by you in their day; and when nighttime comes, they do not even say good night. They do this to you day in and day out. You wait patiently to see if they will see you, and they never do. You wait patiently to see if they will ever show their thankfulness or gratitude for your giving all you had to give them life. Still everybody and everything is much more important than you. And they have the power to pick you up and discover all the things that you left for them, and they put you in your place. They get tempted to come to you, and they quickly make a decision to go to someone else who never loved them. Understand the heartache of watching this day after day. Understand this is exactly what you do with Jesus day in and day out.

Imagine the heartache of watching them suffer and endure things so needlessly when you have all the power to help them, and yet they not only don't see you but also don't want you. They are on the phone all the time with people who do not have the power to help them and do not love them the way you do. Those people compared to your love simply do not care. They say they do, they even think they do, but you know that they can't, and this goes on and on and on.

Imagine that your presence of the few little things that you were able to say or do they make the decision to tie your hands behind your back and put a gag in your mouth in order to keep you in your place on the shelf. This is how Jesus is treated every day and all day long. How long do you honestly think that I will strive to walk and talk with you? How long do you imagine that I will continually wait for you to discover My Word? How much did My Son have to give, more than His life? What would it take to cause you to love Him in His Word? And if you *finally* make a decision to turn toward Him, would I really care? Your whole lifetime did this to My Son. Even as a Christian that attends church faithfully. And yet you expect Me to be there when you pray, when you think, when you feel, when you decide to believe. Who is unfair here? Is it I, or is it you?

Jesus said that "if I be lifted up, I will draw all men unto Me." You run everywhere lifting up others, lifting up yourself, and you wonder why you cannot draw anybody to serve someone that you yourself have been refusing to serve for *years*. To make it easier on you, to see to it that I can reach you or that you will hear and see and love My Son, I sent My Spirit. You go to church and bask in My Presence. You enjoy so much of Me and take it as though you are so good, so wonderful that God chose you to bless. How wonderful the Spirit comes down upon you. After all, you're going to church, and you are so obedient. It was such a tremendous sacrifice. You had to get up earlier than you want to, you had to make yourself presentable, and you have to listen to the Word if you belong to a Bible-preaching church. You sometimes fall asleep, you sometimes judge others, and you look around at what everyone is doing. You find fault with those who love and worship Me. And you make up your mind that you will not return this evening because after all you did your part. You think, "Oh no, here comes the preacher. He might expect me to give my share or do my share." This is your attitude speaking. "Oh, but I am so holy. Haven't I proved it just by coming here? Oh, surely I made points with God today. Oh no, the preacher is speaking about tithing this morning. I will be sure that I will never come back to this church. How dare they tell me what to do with my money?" All these things go on in your mind, and you are sure that they are hid from Me and that you will be able to fool Me the way you fool yourself. And do you honestly believe that if and when you make a decision it just might be too late? Here is My attitude speaking. "I don't think it will ever occur to you."

PART XV

"Why do the heathen rage, and the people imagine a vain thing? The kings of the earth set themselves, and the rulers take counsel together, against the LORD, and against His anointed saying, *Let us break their bands asunder, and cast away their cords from us*" (Psalm 2:1-3).

Nobody wants to hear that they are not where they need to be. As My Word says, only the wise will take a rebuke and use the wisdom to make them wiser. When you are a child and refuse to listen to authority, in your parents you say, "No one is going to tell me what to do." If you have someone to take care of you, when mother and father work, you say, "You're not my mother, you're not my father, I don't have to listen to you." When you go to school, you say, "You're not my boss, I don't have to listen to you." When you grow up, you say, "I don't have to listen to anybody, I am my own boss. I know the difference between good and evil, and I can decide what is good for me." You are eating from the same tree Adam and Eve disobeyed and ate from. And it seems to be as Satan told them that they did not have to listen to God, they could become like God and know the difference between good and evil. But none of you know the difference without My Word. Children, that is why I sent a guide, the Bible, to tell you the difference according to Me as to what is good or evil. The world may seem to be able to reject it, but you cannot afford to.

Some of you are fortunate; you have talents that enable you to come into positions of authority. Some of you live like kings, thinking success is something that is all that a person can or should achieve. Perhaps you've gone on to college by now; and the more you learn, the more you refuse to listen to common sense, the more you refuse to listen to common decency, the more you refuse to listen to anybody or anything that would dare tell you the truth. Now you're an adult and perhaps in a place that you can make decisions that affect the lives of others, and you gather with those who are just like you, and you decide that no book is ever going to dictate to you what is good or bad speaking of the Bible. So you take the only guide I sent and toss it behind you and agree not to permit anyone to ever preach or teach the truth in My Word to you. You began this life rebellious, and you continue even when you are given the Word to change.

Why do the heathen rage? Why is it that so much evil seems to prevail? Why do they imagine a vain thing? Why do those who do not believe that My Son *is* My Son imagine for one minute that they can live without God? Which is a vain thing. Because those whom I called, those whom I chose refuse to allow themselves to be under the authority of Mine anointed. You work very hard to make sure that no one will ever dictate the truth to you. So you do away with public prayer, you do away with the law to not kill helpless human beings. Worse yet, you think because you have never personally done it, and have never really approved of it, as a Christian it will not touch your life. Read Revelations when I spoke to the Laodiceans about not being completely for Me and not being completely against Me. I will spit you out of My mouth, for I would rather have you hot or cold. I tell you right now that when you think for one moment that you can support such a person because they look and sound so good and that it will be all right with Me, you have just seen to it that you have become partaker of evil deeds. You defeat evil. You don't hold its hand, you don't use it to your cause or purpose, and you don't blind your eyes to it and give it power through your hard-earned money. You are to touch not, taste not, and handle not. You as a Christian are called to keep your life clean. How in the world can you expect Me to deliver you out of anything when you are in total agreement with Satan through the people you support? They may win in all they achieve, they may have such a spirit that it looks like I Am with them. I assure you that I Am not. *And if they succeed, I did not give it to them, you did. You just handed your life on a silver platter to the enemy of your soul, and we will see if any man can deliver you. This is not the hour to be looking to men to deliver you, not the hour to be looking for a savior where any part of your life is concerned. Had you read the Word, you would have seen it. You would have recognized the truth. I Am not for or against any party or any group. I Am telling you not to put your trust in anything other than My Word.*

Two cannot walk together unless they agree. If you are in agreement with evil in order to obtain good, Paul the Apostle says that your damnation is just. Let God be true and every man a liar. If anyone comes to you and tells you anything that is not in My Word and you discard My Word and believe them, you are making them true and Me a liar.

Hear what I Am telling you. Certain things will *never mix*. A double tongue will seem to, but I assure you that righteousness will never come from any person no matter who they are that can take human life lightly and then dare say they do not answer to anyone for it. I assure you, you will answer to Me. The heathen can't rage, they can't imagine that they can get away with evil without your support. You are not responsible for their actions, but you are partaker with them, when you see fit to help them. You might as well take something in your hand and defeat your own self. I gave you "Life," in Jesus Christ. He is not an author of death for the unprotected innocent. Adults who make mistakes with their choices should never have the power to destroy the innocent because they do not want to pay the consequences of their own actions. Where in the world is your reasoning as a Christian?

Two can never walk together lest they be agreed. And when you support someone or something that supports same-sex marriages and abortion, I assure you that you can depend on *My Word being fulfilled in your life.* I Am according to My Word continually against those who do such things, and why as someone who calls yourself by My name would I ever let you be partaker of bringing these things to pass? *I will never go against My Word. I will always hate sin.* It is never a matter of whether you believe it or not. It is never a matter of whether you accept it or not. It is never a matter of whether you reject it, embrace it, etc. But it is most definitely a matter of My Word being fulfilled, and I promised that I will fulfill the negative along with the positive, and you cannot embrace the evil without consequences. Look around you, do you see them nipping at your heels?

PART XVI

"And Jesus, immediately knowing in Himself that virtue had gone out of Him, turned about in the press, and said, Who touched My clothes? And His disciples said unto Him, Thou seest the multitude thronging Thee, and sayest Thou, who touched Me?" (Mark 5:30).

Today billions of people throng Jesus every day. All are seeking something from Him. Some need a healing, some need deliverance, some want and desire prosperity and many more things. Virtue went out of Him, and *He felt it*. He was thronged by so many people, and all were striving to touch the hem of His garment, and only one touched Him. *Only one person caught His attention* and caused Him to look around for her. *Just one.* This very incident should speak volumes to you. You can believe that it was her faith that touched Him. But I tell you now that it was more than needing a healing that gave her the faith to be able to believe, and He knew it. He rewarded her with a healing. But He knew that she had touched His very being. She had touched His moral excellence. She had touched the power and the presence of the purity of God. Not because she needed so desperately, although she did.

It was not her faith, but her desire to have God. She had to have been a person who sought God and then believed that He could and would heal her. Her faith had to be that she believed that He had the power to be the author and the finisher of her faith.

You don't see it like that. You do not see that if you desire Jesus the way she did, you can and would touch Him. But you must believe that He is morally excellent, and there are certain things that He would not nor could He ever do. Many are reaching for the prize of the high calling, and many will never obtain it because they accept an unrealistic version of what Jesus Christ is all about. They have diluted Him to be in the confines of their thinking, their feelings, and their ways. Jesus is powerful and limitless and can only be touched by our faith. And faith cannot be born into a soul unless they understand and realize how morally excellent God truly is. This understanding comes by putting the Word in you. *Listen!* If you don't have the desire that it takes to go to God will all of your heart because you love Him and that you are willing to die for Him and you seem to have a power of being blessed or your prayers seem to be answered, it is time for the fear of Me to come upon you to realize how deceived you really are. It is time to permit Me to lead you into the truth, into repentance.

The Bible is truly a mirror, able to reveal your reflection and tell you who you really are. And when you reach up, when you reach out, He can feel and know exactly who you are. He is touched by the feelings of our infirmities. *When we reach up for strength to do His will, that is faith and He is touched.* When we reach up to obtain the power to overcome ourselves, that is faith and He is touched. We can reach up for what we desire and what we want, but it is not always the best thing for us; someone else it touched and helps you continue in deception, and it is not Me. What is the most excellent way is to desire to do His will. Success is never a sign that I Am with you. I bless the just and unjust alike. I give you all breath, I give you all the power to make and get wealth, I give you so many things; and you are foolish enough to believe that because I Am faithful and give, you are where you are supposed to be. That is your mistake, *not Mine;* so if you succeed in the public eye and still do not repent of lying or of killing the innocent, then I Am not with you unless you repent. And those who support you, I Am not with them unless they repent.

He died that you might live, and you are to die to this carnal world and all that goes against the Word so that He might live in you. He gave His life that you would give your life to Him enough to give Him the ability to change it. When you see yourself so much less than what He Himself said you could or would be, *it is you that hinders it.*

Reach today for Him, and be not afraid to ask for His will to be done each and every day. He sees your weaknesses, and He knows who you are, and He lives to help you to overcome them all, not accepting them and living with them, but by getting rid of them and getting them under the blood of Jesus Christ.

PART XVII

"And I saw a great white throne, and him that sat on it, from whose face the earth and the heaven fled away; and there was found no place for them. And *I saw the dead, small and great, stand before God; and the books were opened: and another book was opened, which is the book of life: and the dead were judged out of those things which were written in the books, according to their works*" (Revelation 20:11, 12).

"And whosoever was not found written in the book of life was cast into the lake of fire" (Revelation 20:15).

*J*esus's *own words told you plainly that you will be judged by your words.* Matthew 12:36, 37 (KJV) says, "But I say unto you, that every idle word that men shall speak, they shall give account thereof in the day of Judgment. *For by thy words thou shalt be justified, and by thy words thou shalt be condemned.*" How is it that you take the words of Jesus so lightly? What in the world makes you think that I have not the power to record every word that you have ever spoken? With innumerable angels at My disposal, I record every thought, every word, and every deed. The only escape from judgment comes by your faith in the blood that Jesus shed for you, by your faith to believe that He is your only door to heaven. He plainly told you in His word that

160

He is the door, He is the Way, He is the life. "No man can come to the Father but by Me," He said in John 14:6.

Revelation 20:12 says great and small stand before My Throne. Both small and great and the books will be opened along with the book of life which is the Word, and all will be judged by those things written in the books according to their works.

Just as surely as your life seems to pass by so quickly, you must remember that time cannot be stopped by you. Just as surely as you are headed to the grave the moment you are born. So it is that you are headed for the Judgment. There is only one way to erase all the pages in those books, and it isn't by your good works. It is by faith in the blood of Jesus Christ, the Lamb of God who takes away the sins of the world. When you stand before Me, your priest, your pastor, your neighbor, your spouse, no one will be able to speak for you. Because the books will speak for themselves, and by your own words, you will be justified or condemned. *Think of it, your own words.*

Of all the stages the church has gone through, it has led up to this day that the Holy Spirit has been poured out on all flesh. And yet up ahead, is there any wisdom to see what is coming? Jesus said a wicked and adulterous generation seeks after a sign. Wanting to see ahead that perhaps there is some way to escape what is inevitable in every life.

The one major event before the rapture, before the second coming of Jesus, the church has to go through is judgment. Not at the judgment, but be judged on earth so that you won't be judged at the Judgment. This is why I said that if you judge yourself, no man can judge you. How do you suppose that I meant for you to judge yourself? You are to judge yourself exactly as you will be judged and with the same book. You must take the word to heart and judge your own selves by looking in the mirror of the word and making sure you are obedient. And if you find that you are not, then you are to pray and repent. I promised that if you would turn from your wicked ways and humble yourselves and repent, I would heal your land.

Since you are going to be judged by the word according to your works, then it is reasonable that you have the mirror of the word to see exactly where you stand with Me here on earth so that you will not have to endure any judgment at the Throne. How simple a matter it all is and how simple a message all of it is. I have revealed so much in My Word to keep you safe, I have revealed so much through the gospel to *keep you safe if you will read it.*

I cannot judge the world or deal with anyone in the world until I first deal with My church if they are not where they need to be. This is the warning of your life to come to Jesus and make all things right in My sight by examining yourselves with the Word. Your righteousness is as filthy as rags to Me. How can I accept your good works when My Son gave His life? He did no sin but still gave His life for you to go to heaven through Him. Do you honestly believe that I will sit at the judgment and listen to you say that you had some other way other than the one I provided for you in My Son Jesus? Anything that you can say or do annuls His death and makes it useless. And that is tramping on the great price that He paid.

The Bible is not open for interpretation; it is not for man's wisdom to understand because in man's wisdom, he had no need for Me. Man decided that he knew what was evil and what was good without Me. So I chose the foolishness of preaching the cross as the only way for man to be saved. It isn't true that you are to never ask for anything. Jesus said ask. He paid the way for you to ask. He made the way that if you ask for My Holy Spirit to enlighten your mind and open your understanding, you will know exactly what the word says without any interpretation. But you must believe that I Am so holy, so true that I will never go against one word. I Am not a man that I should lie, nor will I change My mind.

PART XVIII

"But the Comforter, which is the Holy Ghost, whom the Father will send in My name, He shall teach you all things, and bring all things to your remembrance, whatsoever I have said unto you." (John 14:26).

Do you not know that when Jesus died, he promised to send you the Holy Spirit that He may lead you into the Word which is leading you into all truth? Do you not know that if you comfort yourself with any other comfort it is evidence of your going against yourself and hindering yourself? For some of you, it has been handed down through generations to be this way. Check it out and see if what I say isn't so in your life.

Are you wasting your life and talents with things of no profit? Is selfishness so much in your life, centering on no one else but you? The influences of the past capture the weak, and they become alcoholics and drug addicts. Past generations of your life never sincerely searched for God. Your generation is so affected that you have to force yourself to read the Bible, pray, force yourselves to do what you know is right and good for you or your family. Some people overcome these weaknesses, and some don't.

Are you one of those who are always searching for knowledge, information, and understanding, believing that it is power as long as it

163

doesn't come from the Bible? Finding anything to read or watch just so long as it isn't the Bible. Most of the time, as a Christian who attends church faithfully, you feel more of a desire for a television program or movie than getting into the Word, which has the power to save you. Do you not realize that you must pray your way through these temptations and ask Me to set you free from your past generations? These kind of people will accept everything and anything for comfort, for a source of power, just so long as it isn't from the Bible. They want nothing to do with My Word, with My people, with My church, and with the things that are of the Bible.

These kinds of people are always lifting up the wicked, supporting them, holding their hand, as was written in Malachi 3:15. Letting so many things slide by and thinking all will be well in the end. Even their best efforts fall short of My glory or will. Never being in alignment with Me so that they can carry a sincere burden for their spouse, children, church, community, nation, or neighbor. They have to force themselves to pray. And being so self-centered, they think that what little they do is so much more than it really is. And if they do accept some truth, they corrupt it and turn it into idolatry or legalism. Being puffed up with pride, they see themselves better than they are, knowing more than what they do know. In 1 Corinthians 8:2, it says, "And if any man thinks that he knoweth anything, he knoweth nothing yet as he ought to know." Calling themselves Christians, they forget that they need to be easily entreated. They are always ready to fight, to strive, being unthankful, without humility. These are violent people taking the kingdom of God by force. They worship singers, movie stars, and any kind of players just so long as it isn't the Living God spoken about in the Word.

All of these things that you turn to, you turn seeking comfort, when I sent you a comforter. Understand how wicked this is for you to claim Jesus Christ, and you run to everyone and everything else for comfort that can only come through the presence of the Holy Spirit.

These allow their money to slip through their fingers and buy what they don't need without any intention of paying for it, thinking it will drop from heaven somehow, no matter how deep in debt they become.

These things are all generational. You get depressed because you have allowed yourself to spend more than you should. You do that because you think if you buy something, it will make you feel better. Ever notice how a family is blessed and has peace and is able to do the right things and how another one seems to always be in trouble or have trouble? You need to learn about past generations enough to make sure you do not give in to these influences, for the world calls it genetic, but it has to be generational before it affects the genetics, and many need to pray for their children and their children's children.

It isn't your nerves that cause you to abuse your children verbally or physically. It is the fact that you have no natural affection. You want to know why? Read Romans chapter 1 and learn how I revealed everything to you, and you still refuse the truth. Some of you go home in this condition after church, and you keep going as though you are not doing these things because you do not know how to be free. You have part of the gospel but not all. The only way to be free is to repent of believing that somehow it will all be all right and start believing the Word and pray for a desire to change into the vessel you are called to be. Some of you don't do this because it is too much like work. Why do you think I told you to work out your salvation with fear and trembling?

You have become faultfinders, scorners, witches, gossipmongers, liars, cheaters and stealers; and the worst of you abide in church devouring all other churches, seeking to get yourselves proselytes in your church. Since you don't believe in miracles, then you cannot believe that I can and will free you. You don't believe My Word that when the Son of God sets you free, ye shall be free indeed. I Am still working miracles today and each and every day. And the greatest miracle is the one that I do when I operate on the soul that seeks to change. And all the while you claim to be searching for God, claim to be seeking Him when you turn Him away each and every day.

Some of you know the Word, and you know exactly how to strive, fight, and argue the Word, but you do not know how to live the Word. You recognize all the sins in others but never look at yourself in the mirror of the Word. I promised to send strong delusion to those who do not receive the love of the truth. In 2 Thessalonians 2:11-12 it says, "And

165

for this cause God shall send them strong delusion, that they should believe a lie, that they all might be damned who believed not the truth, but had pleasure in unrighteousness." Because you don't love the truth, you don't believe the truth, and you won't receive the truth, and you have pleasure in unrighteousness, you have troubles and problems today.

I hear the cry of Mine anointed, they are those preachers that are great men and women of God, those who are determined that they will deliver the truth at any cost. I told you plainly in the Word that he who preaches and teaches to obey My commandments is great in the kingdom of heaven. Your cry is not the one I will hear when you need Me, for you did not hear My cry through them when they preached on tithing and offerings and obedience. You decided long ago to be the fool who doesn't really believe that there is a God and that My Word is true. You didn't want anyone to know it or see it, so you sit every Sunday in the pew.

Even those who refuse to go to church, who refuse to read their Bible, who trouble My people are better off than you. Because they know where they are at, no one has to tell them where they are going, but you, you have made yourself so blind that no message could ever reach you.

To be able to repent will not be a one-time trip to the altar or one dip on your knees. Because the sin you have chosen will not be so easy to get rid of. The day that I in My great mercy called you, you refused to hear. You will now have to work to get there, and in so doing, you will prove to Me that I can trust you with the truth. You will prove to Me that you will never again go after idols, that you will never again destroy anyone. I have not a hammer raised up ready to come down on you hard for every mistake. I only come down hard on those who are hard on others. You are going to have to come to Me and seek out through the Word all the sins that led you astray, and that will take time and effort, not just one drop at the altar and a few tears to be shed. My Word is true, your sins will find you out, and they will follow you to the judgment, and they will not be that easy to get rid of as they once were when you were first called.

People like you are in a great number sitting in the pews doing nothing to obey My Word, and you have given the devil power to run rampant over this nation through leadership that destroys the innocent and approves of men with men and women with women. You give them power by not being where you need to be in order to pray and intercede for this great nation. You think that these people are worthy of hell, but what have you done that is any better? Most of them know who and what they are, but do you? I do. I watch you judge them, condemn them, talk about them, and then turn on the television and completely enjoy them; and because you are ignorant of Me, and do not see Me or hear Me, you vote for someone who support the things that I hate.

When you go into the Word, it is the Holy Spirit that guides you when you need to be comforted. You experience great peace and joy because of My comforting presence. This daily time of being with the Word was intended to be used to comfort you. If you are told by a doctor that a loved one is dying and there is no hope, My Word is for your comfort through My presence of My Spirit to remind you that nothing is impossible with Me. Just as surely as you take the positive of it, you must be warned of the negative.

PART XIX

"Wherefore whosoever shall eat this bread, and drink this cup of the Lord, unworthily, shall be guilty of the body and blood of the Lord. But let a man examine himself, and so let him eat of that bread and drink of that cup. For he that eateth and drinketh unworthily, eateth and drinketh damnation to himself, not discerning the Lord's body. For this cause many are weak and sickly among you and many sleep. For if we would judge ourselves, we should not be judged. But when we are judged, we are chastened of the Lord, that we should not be condemned with the world" (1 Corinthians 11:27-32).

I have told you repeatedly that the Word is Jesus and that you must eat and drink the Word. I have reminded you that He is the bread of life. Everyone with even a little bit of knowledge understands communion. But can you see the communion that you have with the Word of God? Can you see that you can eat the Word and drink the Word unworthily and bring damnation to yourself? And that for this cause many are weak and sickly among you and many sleep?

Using the Word for self-seeking purposes, and using it to curse your enemies and do good to yourself and to believe that I Am with you no matter what the cause you have in mind is, is as unworthily as you can get. When you are sinning in your heart and do not have Jesus living within there and are focused on your own purposes and agenda, you are using the Word which is Jesus to do your bidding unworthily, not discerning the Lord's body and the Lord's blood. You are actually eating and drinking damnation to yourself. Ask yourself a question, what have you done with My Word that I should serve you? Don't you realize that I do not serve you, that I Am not here to answer your prayers and do your bidding? If you pick up the word and read it, you are feeding off of the bread of life which is His body. And I warn you now that if you take this book and use it to point the finger at any part of My body which is the church, you will answer to Me. For this book is written to them in love, to cause them to see which direction to go in an hour that is unlike any other.

> *Every day you ask Me to forgive your debts or trespasses. And every day you accept that you are a sinner, and you make the blood of Jesus Christ look like nothing because you never seek Him to lead you to repentance of those sins that you know you commit every day. You say that you have faith and you use that faith for everything but freedom from sin.*

You don't think this is true? Confess to Me then that you know that you are in My will. Oh, you're afraid of Me. How does that work? How can you be afraid of Me and still sin against Me by not obeying My Word? Oh, you think that I truly could not possibly have meant that you obey and that I would understand when you tramp on the blood of Jesus and render it as nothing. Just toss it behind you the way you are supposed to toss the world, the flesh, and the devil. When you toss it, you will see that it is a fearful thing to fall into the hands of the Living God. I Am not a dead, do-nothing God. I Am alive and well, and if you ever look in the back of My book, you would know how the story ends.

This message is not for the obedient; I have great men and women who preach to those. It is for the lawless, the unbelieving, the fearful, and the abominable, to give them one chance to repent. Oh, that's not you. Ha. You will see Me laugh when I visit. I Am talking to those who go to church by the millions and claim the Holy Spirit within them. That very same Holy Spirit that you claim within you has the power through the Word to completely pull you out of sin. All you have to do is fall to your knees every time you see that your life, your thoughts, your ways do not line up to the Word. My grace is so sufficient to help if you ask. Think about it, the only things you ever truly asked for were for things or to do things or for your favorite football team or your favorite idol of any kind or when you or yours were sick or in need of someone you know or someone that you hear about on television after the tragedy. It is then too late to pray. Because you do not look ahead to protect Me in others, are you sure that I will look ahead and protect you? Some of you are motivated to pray simply because you are so afraid that if you don't pray, your child could be next. Where is your love? Can you not see that little ones need your prayers before they are kidnapped? And that these people who act like animals need to be caught quickly.

I know, I know, you take the scripture that all things work together for good to them that love God. Well, if you are doing wrong and looking for an answer from Me, and you never truly believe that you can do wrong, you can be so deceived that you continue to believe that I Am working it all out and even claim it, but that doesn't make it so. Things happen, and you continue to use the word to take the consequences of your actions off of you and put them on someone else when you are wrong.

Some of you have listened to messages over and over and over and never move to repentance or obedience, and because I have not corrected you yet and I have blessed you, you actually believe that I Am with you when you are so wrong. I Am under no obligation to bless, deliver, or heal any one of you who insists that I Am like you, that I would do the evil things that you would do.

PART XX

"Who knowing the judgment of God that they, which commit such things are worthy of death, not only do the same but have pleasure in them that do them" (Romans 1:32).

Now don't get this wrong and say that I hate homosexuals because I do not. I hate sin, not people. Those of you who have the audacity to speak for Me and tell these people that I hate them come under the power of the Word which says in Romans chapter 2. You can see someone else is given up to sin, but can you see where you are given up to sin? Are you God that you can tell how and why a person is in their condition? And are you God that you are permitted to enjoy your television and movies and judge those you enjoy watching?

You condemn yourselves and prove that you have no natural affection for anyone. It is natural not to be so cruel or mean to someone and tell them they are hated when they are dying or suffering the loss of their loved one. Many of these people live better as people than you do. All the principles of My Word is fulfilled in some of them. They actually live better than you do They strive to be kind and do what is right according to their knowledge. They don't fight, hate, and condemn you. I Am not speaking for all of them; I Am only telling you

171

that if you commit one sin, it measures up to theirs if you are saved by you not sinning. I said not one sin will enter into heaven; and if you read Romans chapter 1, you will see that I measure sin as the same, with only commas in between each and every sin. You measured out that one sin was worse than the other. One sin has worse consequences here on earth. But all sin has the same eternal consequence. So if you judge them to be going to hell, when I said don't judge, then you are measuring out your own judgment.

The evil of your own hearts desires to hide your own sins enough to point the finger at others, and this keeps you from ever looking in your own heart and asking Me to search you. How are any of you any better than they that you dare to judge anyone? While you praise me at church, you devour your children and your spouse and scream and yell and strive and fight because you desire only your way. They submit to one another and strive to be kind while many of you are so entangled over some doctrine of length of skirts, signs of the cross, wearing of pants in church, etc. How many of you are watching your neighbor's faults and puffing yourselves up with pride one against another? Shall I not visit these sins? They are worse than the worlds because you claim that I Am with you in the doing of them.

PART XXI

"For God so loved the world, that He gave His only begotten Son, that whosoever believeth in Him should not perish, but have everlasting life. For God sent not His Son into the world to condemn the world; but that the world through Him might be saved. He that believeth on Him is not condemned; but he that believeth not is condemned already, because he hath not believed in the name of the only begotten Son of God. And this is the condemnation, that light is come into the world, and men loved darkness rather than light, because their deeds were evil. For every one that doeth evil hateth the light, neither cometh to the light, lest his deeds should be reproved. *But he that doeth truth cometh to the light, that his deeds may be made manifest, that they are wrought in God*" (John 3:16-21).

Heart, O heart, how long will you go against yourself? How long will you put Me off and determine yourself to destroy yourself without the truth within Me? I Am the Spirit of Truth, and I will reveal to you the truth. In an hour that a man or a woman faces death, their whole life sometimes flashes before them as I speak to them about the things they have done wrong. Some of you

173

laugh at this, and some mock at this truth, but that flash is a moment in time to cause you to repent, for you to see that you are going to stand before Me and to cause you to humble yourself before Me. To cause you to admit under My mighty hand where you are wrong, and perhaps I will consider to spare you for another chance to make all things right. For if all isn't made right, you have no chance at all. If you have experienced an accident in which you know everything went into slow motion, it was Me giving you plenty of time to repent and talk to Me. What will you do with your second chance?

Some of you promised Me over and over that you would serve Me, and as soon as the problem is gone and you are delivered, you forget to serve Me. That service begins by getting into My Word and learning of Me. I Am a God of second chances, understanding the hardness of your hearts that you do not want to come to the light because you do not want to be told by anybody that you are wrong or could be wrong. But if you do not humble yourself here, you will have no opportunity to repent at the Throne.

You live with a man or a woman without being married. You talk to Me and try to take advantage of Me the way you have been able up until now; you manipulate things to suit yourself and believe that because you confess I gave you a special dispensation of the gospel and because I know exactly where you are at I will somehow go against My Word and not hold you responsible for your choices. When you have had years to rethink and repent, and you still refuse to believe that I Am true to My Word and always will be, you are deliberately making Me look like a liar; and I assure you that I Am not with you. Anytime you continue in the sin that you know is a sin, know this, I will never go against My Word. If a man knows to do good and doeth it not to him, it is a sin.

Many have found themselves in your shoes for whatever reasons, perhaps not living together while you are unmarried. Some turned their back on Me, and because My Word promises that I will never leave you or forsake you, you take it as though I condone or approve of your sin. I Am there waiting for you to repent. Many, all the while they were in that sin, did not justify themselves, did not lie on Me and say that I gave a special dispensation of the gospel to them. They got the victory and were won back to me because they cried out daily that they knew it was a sin and that they did not want to be like that; they did not want to continue because they knew that it would lead away from Me. Do not be so foolish as to think that I will not require obedience to My Word. Do not be so foolish as to think that I will cause so many to repent and not you. I urge you to repent, I urge you to cry out to Me to change this evil way of thinking that I would ever go against My word. Jesus paid too huge a price for Me to allow you to continue and have peace in the sin you know is wrong.

Please listen! For your sake, I urge you to consider what is being said here. Understand that although I love you, I will never permit one soul to do these things. Strong delusion is the end result, and I do send it so that you would believe a lie because you have not received the love of the truth.

PART XXII

"But the hour cometh, and now is, when the true worshippers shall worship the Father in Spirit and in truth: for the Father seeketh such to worship Him. God is a Spirit and they that worship Him must worship Him in Spirit and in truth" (John 4:23 KJV).

In church you have some very faithful. You call them the more spiritual ones. God seems to be for them and not for you. They faithfully read their Bibles, and they pray and watch over their souls and the souls of others, and still you look at them as though they are some strange creature that surely God did not intend for you. When all of you do become like that in church and at home, there will be no stopping My voice. In order to get there, it begins with you.

I am not speaking of the ones who necessarily dance before Me, sing before Me, prophesy, or even have gifts of healings. I Am talking about those who live and breathe Me twenty-four seven, who are never overwhelmed because they learned how to give all things to Me, who are never upset because they learned how to walk content in all things. You know those who have love, joy, peace, long-suffering, temperance, and meekness. Those who never change because of circumstances, situations of life, those who shine with My glory. You know the ones you have sat and ate with or worshipped with that you thought for sure that you never had to be like them for they were close with God and you just didn't need to be. You live off of their prayers when you have needs, and yet you never desire to walk and talk with Me the way they do.

Matthew 13:45, 46 (KJV) says, "Again the kingdom of heaven is like unto a merchant man, seeking pearls: who when he had found one pearl of great price, went and sold all that he had and bought it."

Most of the time between Me and the vessel that is writing this book is a time that we never speak. *It is a constant flow of revelation.* I reveal to her exactly how I feel; and she, spirit to Spirit, reveals to Me exactly how she feels. That language of love that We have toward one another is now equalized on both sides. Of course she cannot love Me the way I do her because I Am God. When I say equalized, it is as much as she is capable of and as much as I Am capable of. You see, she *allowed* Me to love her so much that I now flow through her, and the love is now returned to Me. She walks in heaven here on earth for we now are together forever. No circumstance, no situation ever comes up that this is not shared between us. There is never a time now that she cannot or doesn't hear Me. There is never a time that I cannot and do not hear her because We are so close. She sees Me now as I Am, and I see her now as she is. There is no hiding; there is no deception between us. It is love on love, love in love, love to love. When I communicate with you in the Spirit, spirit to Spirit, there is no need for words. As long as she is in the human, she will always use words, but between us there is no real need. I use words because I understand that she is still in the flesh, but we are so close that when her time comes to leave this earth, there will be no moment of separation.

She found a treasure, a pearl of great price in My Son, and I found a treasure in her. There are those of you who value her, and I was not disappointed in you, for I knew that you would. There are those who dismissed her as nothing because you seem so great. But one of the things that kept her going was those who were in need so much that they valued her and honored her. I could tell you so much more because I have so many books about her. That when heaven greets her for all to see, it will be written across heaven what she enabled Me to do in her life.

You see, many of you have a part, and you are not doing it. She calls it your homework. You expect Me to do it all for you. I commune with her the way I did with Adam in the garden, the way I did with Jesus when He had so few words to say, but when He spoke, He was powerful in Me.

Sometimes being in the human, she makes mistakes, and I always reveal them to her before any of it can bring any real harm to her or anyone else. I have written, and I Am writing all this that you may clearly see an example of what I had intended to have with everyone who is willing to let Me walk and talk with them. This book practically repeats itself to make sure that the communication with Me is all according to my Word so that you will not enter into deception. I cannot tell it enough. I cannot say it enough, for there are those who would love to imitate it; and try as they might, they cannot. The secret of the relationship is not in you, it is in Me; and I do not give it to anyone who claims it, I give it to someone that I choose to have it. This relationship grows, and as it grows, her spirit prospers, and as her spirit prospers, so does My Presence within her.

The last time the enemy attacked her and tried to give her a heart attack, she was in tremendous pain in her left arm and her jaw and her chest; and she was terribly weak, unable to function. As she lay on the bed, she could see Me clearly sitting on the edge of the bed, stroking her head the way a mother would push back the hair and stroke the head of a sick child. I said, "You're going to be all right, and I want you to do something for Me. I want you to get up in the name of Jesus right now and walk on into the things you have to do. Don't let the enemy keep you in this physical condition." Immediately as always, she obeyed and got up instantly; and since she had no strength and it seemed like she would fall over and pass out, she simply walked in the name of Jesus Christ. She walked into the kitchen and said to her husband that she was going to finish washing clothes. He tried to talk her out of it, and she said, "I will do this in the name of Jesus." And since her washing machine was outside, she went out on the deck and slowly went down the steps one at a time. She did exactly what I said; she resisted the enemy's power over her and then one by one went back up the steps.

She then called her college pastor and agreed with him for a restoration of the heart, and instantly everything disappeared.

Some of you have come this far because you have the Word abiding within you, and you have allowed the Holy Spirit within you to become what I created you to be. And some of you will realize what you have as you read this. And you will see Me grow quickly within you. All that you know about My Word will come alive and be quickened as soon as I see and know that I can trust you with everything.

I will also tell you now that some of you are afraid to approach Me in this manner. She was for a long, long time. But as I worked with her through My fear, she was able to recognize Me more easily and know that it is impossible to imitate My Spirit. Even though the enemy has the power to change into an angel of light, he has not the power to change into Me.

Perfect love casts out all fear. As you are given this warning throughout this book, you can pray that I do visit you the way I did her that you may know Me the way I Am, not the way you make Me out to be. This will enable Me to cleanse and keep you close to Me at all times. Romans chapter 8 is true, that I will not condemn you the moment you step toward Me, that I will help you overcome everything.

PART XXIII

I want to finish this up with this, for it is a portrait of My love for her. It shows exactly how I felt the moment she had the victory and was no longer in the bondage of the enemy. I waited many years because when I found her, she was mentally and emotionally ill. She would run and try to bash her head into a tree full force, and with My mighty hand only a second before her head would have hit, I threw her backward about seven feet. She would land on her bottom and get up and again run full force, with her head down to bash her head into a tree. And I would do it again, and she would land on her bottom. Because she could not bear what her mind was going through. To live through her life just one twenty-four-hour period was agonizing, and she had nowhere to turn, no one to help her. She could communicate how she felt to no one. She would bash her head into the walls and the floor and then throw her whole body into the walls. And she always said that padded cells were made for her. When she could not endure any longer, she would then strive with all she had to kill herself. To describe what it was like to be her would be impossible. To understand My compassion for her, you could never ever understand no matter how hard you tried. And *nothing* that you could ever imagine could enlighten you to what it must have been like for her to live through one agonizing day. She was seeing things, hearing things, feeling things that drove her right out of her mind at the age of twenty-four. She lived like this until she was thirty-one years old, and I brought the Word to her.

No one else but her and Me, and I would speak to her about it. Someone told her that the things she saw were in the Bible, and she asked them, "What's a Bible?" She was like a wild creature that she had saved one time. A wild rabbit that refused to eat because it was terrified, and she force-fed it. This was what it was like for Me to feed her the things she needed in the beginning.

I took her in hand and became her mental health. I would speak to her about her mind and led her out of it like a maze. Each and every day she was in My Word, listening to Me direct her mind, and I healed her slowly like no doctor ever could. No one knew or understood what went on in that brain because although she did not hide her condition, she did not know she had one, and everyone did not care enough to know. Everyone around her claimed to be saved, and none of them ever told her about Jesus. And there were those, when they saw her suffer, who were so self-righteous they would think, "She asked for it, she deserved it." And nothing could have been further from the truth. Because those individuals who had a sound mind enough to get into the Word and do what they should have done will never be able to say those words to me without Me saying when they suffer those same words. They will ring in your ears. So I had to come to her personally without anyone or any church. When she was healed, she was determined that no one would ever suffer like that as long as she was around, for she would always tell everyone about Jesus, and she does. So when you read this, you will understand exactly how I felt and why:

The day the prisoners were released, My eyes scanned across the multitude of prisoners. There were so many, and they were a sea of faces. But none of them recognized Me. And then our eyes met. We recognized each other. I ran to her, and I lifted her up in My arms, and I held her high the way a parent would run to a child who was tortured for so long, the way a husband would run to his wife. I embraced her with a love that she had never known. With My arm around her shoulder, we walked away, and I paused for a moment, and I looked at her, and I saw that although what she had been through was humanly impossible to overcome, the agonizing torture in her mind should have killed her. She had not changed one bit; the beauty of My Son was so bright within her that she glowed with His presence. There was no memory of pain, no memory of wrong, no memory of anything within her. I held her head between My hands, and I caressed her face as I looked deep into her eyes, and all I could *see was Me.*

I cannot describe to you how it felt to know that all she had gone through had not changed her love for Me. So we walked on, and to her, it was like heaven on earth as we walked hand in hand. I had so many things to tell her, and she had so many things to tell Me, and sometimes I would pause and kiss her hand and look deep into those loving eyes.

Could you imagine what I Am saying here? Can you picture in your mind what it means to Me to know that she had so little to comprehend, so little to understand, so little ability to do anything, but she had a great capacity to love Me? I set all those others free, but they did not recognize Me when I visited them. I was looking for her in that multitude and *she touched Me.*

A WORD FROM THE AUTHOR

I have been through many more tremendous things in my life that are not written in this book. They are too many to write. God's hand has been so much upon me, and everything written in these pages are actual experiences that I had between me and God. I would never dare to claim that I am perfect, nor would I be so foolish as to claim that I am any different than any one of you. I have the same exact Holy Spirit that each of us was given at conversion of the soul to enable us to overcome the wiles of the enemy, our flesh, and the world. God says that He gave every person a measure of faith. To me, that meant that everyone has the same measure that I have since He is not a respecter of persons. And although there is such a gift of faith, and there are so many different gifts, I have always believed that God intended for each of us to exercise our faith to bring it to the fullest potential.

This is why the covenant between Jesus and me was and is so important. The promise to me was that if I let Him guide and direct me, He would bring me to a place that I would be safe from the temptation to turn my back on Him for any reason and that I would never choose my own way. Since I had seen so many fall into temptation and it seemed to become a habit with them. I saw so many destroy their personal lives and live as though God did not exist for them. I became terrified when I was called that my end would be the same. So I prayed that if He would help me and if He would teach me how to never fall into what I had seen, I would keep my end of the promise.

Many times I almost fell forever under the pressure of so many things taking place in my life all at once and for such a long length of time. But always was His wonderful hand there to lift me up. The despair, the temptation to become so discouraged would be so great that I would simply fall as deep as a person could fall and want to die. But His hand was so powerful that He simply reached down and lifted me up in seconds out of that depression and loneliness and taught me how not to ever focus on myself.

Even today as I go to Him, I go with the knowledge that I have done nothing to ever deserve all the wonderful things that He did and does for me even today. Spirit to Spirit, He knows exactly how I feel that the only reason He did all of these things is that He is so faithful. When He uses my hand to heal and touch someone and I see them go under the power of the Holy Spirit, I marvel even today that He chose me for such a miracle. I may never get over marveling at His wonderful love and mighty works. At least I hope that I never do and that it will always be as fresh and new as He makes it for me today.

I have always known that I would write a book. I know even now that there are many more books within Me. My desire is that if this book benefits one soul, then I am blessed. Never did I dream that God would write the book for me. I was always concerned that someone would lift me up to be higher than what I am. I am no different than you. I am no more able, no nobler, no more anything. What you have I have, and what I have you have. The only difference is that I enabled Him to live within me and through me because I was in such a desperate need of love.

Some have said to me, "But look at your faith, how tremendous it is." I can only say that when God distributed faith to everyone, He gave the same measure. He gave different callings, different gifts, but the same exact amount of the Holy Spirit. He gave the same Word, which amounts to the exact same amount of Jesus Christ. He gave access to the Throne to everyone liberally. I used mine. *I* in the beginning *had to*; otherwise, I would have been dead. I always thought of myself as an emergency for God because I was on the brink of losing my mind forever, losing my soul forever, and losing the functioning of the temple that He gave to us all. I don't know why He chose me. And it sometimes hurts that He did because I see so many that do not have what I have. I see so many that are deceived and think they do, and they operate in a spirit that is not of God. The way I used to, because I know all about it, that is how I came here to this place, I learned all these things especially where God will never go, what He will never do. That is so important because if you know that, you have a great handle on keeping deception out of your life.

My relationship with Him is no different than what you make your relationship with Him to be. To this day, I have to work at it daily to endure to the end. Nothing written within these pages causes me to ever think that because I have been through so much, or understand so much, it gives me a pass from enduring and overcoming today. I tell people all the time that they were never with me in my prayer closet as I cried out for God to help me in my unbelief. Many of you have far more faith within you than I did. Many of you have a sounder mind than what I began with. Many of you only think you have problems and troubles. And because you do not seek Him, or use what He has given you in the Word, you waste a precious life. We have only one life to live on this earth for Him. I am determined to die if I have to so that I can hear, "Job well done."

I keep a constant watch over my soul that it not be corrupted by the world, the flesh, or the devil. I have to reach up and touch the hem of His garment for that virtue that can only flow out of Him. I believed in Him from the moment that I heard because never before did I ever know anyone who is so good, so kind, so understanding, so patient, so loving, so giving, so selfless, so much of every good thing that there could be, and so powerful. I fell in love with Him, and I pray that nothing ever erases that love that I have for Him. I know that I am the only one who could do that.

I pray that my attitude, "If I die, I die, but I refuse to give the enemy the glory," never dies. Most of all I pray that everyone who has read this book see themselves as they really are, for in seeing myself as I really am enabled me to have a desire to change. I pray that God give you the desire to be like Him so much that you want nothing more than to die for Him that He might live within you. I pray that He do for you what He did for me and that He will always be your love as He is my love, your husband the way He is my husband, your mother the way He is my mother, your father the way He is my father, your sister the way He is my sister, your brother the way He is my brother, your neighbor the way He is my neighbor, and your friend the way He is my friend. I pray that the hope to see His wonderful face keep us always in Him. Because no one can ever truly be your mother, your father, your sister, your brother, your husband or wife, and your friend the way that He can.

I pray that you never pick up the Word unworthily. That you always keep in mind the souls that trouble you because they are not like you; God intends that you let your light shine enough that you can be used to see them saved. I pray that you realize that nothing comes easy. That although God promised to be with you, to save you, to heal you, and to deliver you, you still must do your part. I pray that you have the courage to turn your back on the world and get into Jesus through the Word and get to know Him so well that you will always be obedient.

I suggest that if you want to read the footnotes of this book, then you read from the book of Matthew straight through to the end of Revelation. For in there you will find all you need to understand the references in this book.

Read about the prophets in Ezekiel, Jeremiah, Isaiah, and so much more.

Also if you belong to a church that doesn't teach salvation and they only teach religion (teaching you religion is when they tell you that in order for you to have God, you must obey their religion), I suggest that you begin to look for a place where they preach and teach the Bible. Because in John 1:1 it says, "In the beginning was the Word and the Word was with God and the Word was God." It tells you plainly that the Bible is the Word which is Jesus Christ and if you read it and pray that it live and breathe within you, Jesus will take up residence in your heart. That you realize that none of us can be positive that we will live as long as tomorrow and that today is the day that you need to give your life to Jesus so that He can become your personal Savior. You ask Him to come into your heart and cover all of your sins with His blood. How He does this is by you reading the Word and as you see where you have done your own thing, gone your own way. You pray and ask for forgiveness, they are then covered by His blood forever. Then ask Him for His Holy Spirit to give you the grace and the power never to do it again. And that grace will come as you continue in the Word and let it do an operation in your heart and in your mind. And you need to begin in the New Testament. Ask Him for His Holy Spirit to lead and guide you into the Bible and, as He promised, lead you into all truth.

Always take the Bible with you when you go to church and see if what they are preaching and teaching is in it. Do they believe that Jesus Christ is the Son of God? Do they believe that He died for us and rose from the grave? Do they believe that the Bible is the infallible Word of God? There is so much more to it than can be written here. But if your heart is sincere, and your desire is for Jesus to come into your life, I promise you that will happen, for He is true to His Word, and He will make a way for you to find a church that will preach the gospel which is the good news of your salvation.

But stay away from people who preach and teach and do not live what they preach and teach, for the Word says you will know them by their fruits. Although you are not permitted to judge any man, you are permitted to examine his or her fruits. I Am not speaking about those who do so many foolish and hard-to-understand things within the body of Christ, for you must remember that we are all human and we all make mistakes.